THE WAY OF LIFE

ZACHARIAS TANEE FOMUM

D1360261

Published
by
CHRISTIAN PUBLISHING HOUSE
ztfbooks@cmfionline.org
https://ztfbooks.com

Unless otherwise stated, the Bible quotations in this book are from the **Revised Standard Version** of the holy Bible, the British edition.

CONTENTS

PREFACE

This book, *"The Way of Life"* being the first book in the series, has as its theme, the Way into the Christian Life - the Way into Jesus Christ - the Way into God - the Way of Life.

It is written specially to help you to find the Lord Jesus, give yourself to Him, and then you will truly begin to live. As you begin to read, we encourage you to press on right to the end and also answer all the questions at the end of each chapter.

Our prayer is that, by the time you finish reading it, you will have entered into a living relationship with Jesus and then you, too, can say, *"Jesus is my Saviour."*

May God bless you very richly!

Yaounde, 1982

Zacharias Tanee FOMUM
B.P. 6090 Yaounde
CAMEROON

THE OLD CREATION

The Bible says,

"If any one is in Christ, he is a new creation; the old has passed away, behold, the new has come" (II Corinthians 5:17).

This verse tells us that there are two creations the old and the new. We shall consider the old creation first.

GOD'S ORIGINAL PURPOSE

God's original purpose was that there might be only one creation, His perfect creation. To accomplish this purpose, He created a perfect world to begin with. In describing God's original creation, the Bible says,

"God saw everything that he had made, and behold, it was very good" (Genesis 1:31).

If God's verdict on a thing was that it was very good, then, it must have been truly good in every sense. The whole creation, including man, was, therefore, perfect at creation. God's heart was satisfied.

WHY GOD CREATED MAN

Man was God's special creation. He was created with four main purposes in view. First of all, he was created to be specially related to God. He was created for special fellowship with God-to be able to enter into a special relationship with God, feel God's feelings and satisfy God's heart. In order for man to be able to do this, God made him very special from the very beginning. He created him in His image and in His likeness. The Bible says,

> "*Then God said, 'Let us make man in our image, after our likeness; and let them have dominion over the fish of the sea, and over the birds of the air, and over the cattle, and over all the earth, and over every creeping thing that creeps upon the earth*'" (Genesis 1:26).

Secondly, man was created for dominion. When he satisfied God's heart by being specially related to Him, he would have dominion over the rest of creation. To put it in other words, man was to willingly submit himself to be ruled, dominated by God, and he would in turn be enabled by God to have dominion over the rest of creation. The original purpose of God was that man should have limitless dominion over the rest of creation. He was to be in authority.

Thirdly, man was to subdue the earth, till the garden and keep it.

> "*And God blessed them, and God said to them, 'Be fruitful and multiply, and fill the earth and subdue it; and have dominion over the fish of the sea and over the birds of the air and over every living thing that moves upon the earth*'" (Genesis 1:28).

> "*The Lord God took the man and put him in the garden of Eden to till it and keep it*" (Genesis 2:15).

In order to subdue, man had to work hard. God never had any thought that man would be lazy. God has always been against laziness.

Fourthly, man was to obey God. The special relationship between God and man was to continue on the grounds of man rendering obedience to God. If that obedience was not forthcoming, everything would break up and be shattered. If man disobeyed God, he would also lose his power over the rest of creation. Obedience is normally tested by commandments. The Bible says,

> "*And the Lord God commanded the man, saying, 'You may freely eat of every tree of the garden; but of the tree of the knowledge of good and evil you shall not eat, for in the day that you eat of it you shall die'*" (Genesis 2:16-17).

So everything was centred around obedience. Man could obey or disobey. The choice was his. He was given freedom by God to do as he liked.

MAN BECOMES AN OLD CREATION

MAN'S SIN

God said to Adam,

> "*Eat of all the trees of the garden except one*" (Genesis 2:17).

It was freedom being given to him to eat as freely as he wished. I do not know how many trees there were in that garden, but I believe that the number was without limit. The choice before Adam was great. God gave only one exception. Only one tree was forbidden to Adam, and it was forbidden in very strong terms: "If you eat of it, you will die that very day." Man did not need to disobey. He was not starving for food, so that the only opening for him was the forbidden fruit. He simply decided that he would do what he wanted. He disobeyed God and ate of the forbidden tree. The Bible says,

> "*So when the woman saw that the tree was good for food, and that it was a delight to the eyes, and that the tree was to be desired to*

make one wise, she took of its fruit and ate; and she also gave some
to her husband, and he ate" (Genesis 3:6).

This was a wilful act. It was not done in ignorance. Man knew what he was doing. He deliberately decided that he knew better than God, and that he wanted independence from God. In that act, man sinned, for sin is choosing one's own way instead of God's way. It is doing that which one knows one should not do and leaving undone what one knows one ought to do.

In committing sin, Adam deliberately chose a pathway of development that was entirely his own. He went wrong from then on, and everything in creation went wrong with him.

THE CONSEQUENCES OF ADAM'S SIN: BROKEN FELLOWSHIP WITH GOD.

Immediately Adam sinned, he fell out of fellowship with God. He became afraid of God and began to hide. There was no longer any place in his heart for the light of God. Immediately he ate the fruit, he died. He did not die physically immediately. He died spiritually immediately, and he would die physically eventually. Spiritual death is separation from God. It is broken fellowship with God.

Adam was cut off from fellowship with God and driven away from God's presence.

"He drove out the man; and at the east of the garden of Eden he placed
the cherubim, and a flaming sword which turned every way, to
guard the way to the tree of life" (Genesis 3:24).

Man, now away from God, was to go the way of increasing spiritual decay and physical disintegration and, finally, ultimate death would come when man would be thrown into the lake of fire, "hell." Hell is the maximum separation from God. It is maximum death. Everyone who is separated from God is already dead spiritually.

Lost dominion over the rest of creation

In cursing the serpent for his part in the sin tragedy, God indicated that dominion was lost, if not in full, then, at least in part; for He said,

> "I will put enmity between you and the woman, and between your seed and her seed; he shall bruise your head, and you shall bruise his heel" (Genesis 3:15).

Instead of man having dominion over the serpent, there was enmity now introduced. From then on, there was to be aggression from creatures that before would have been submissive. Accidents, earthquakes, floods, etc, are all a manifestation of the rebellion of creation against rebellious man.

The whole process of subduing the earth became more laborious

God had said to rebel Adam,

> "Cursed is the ground because of you; in toil you shall eat of it all the days of your life; thorns and thistles it shall bring forth to you; and you shall eat the plants of the field. In the sweat of your face you shall eat bread" (Genesis 3:17-19).

The earth was no longer normal after the rebellion of Adam. It brought forth thorns and thistles. These were not in the original creation. Mosquitoes that need the blood of man to survive evolved and the earth became a less habitable place.

Instead of being God's co-labourer, man was degraded, demoted

God said to fallen Adam,

> "... till you return to the ground, for out of it you were taken; you are dust, and to dust you shall return" (Genesis 3:19).

I can feel something of the pain that God must have felt when He made that pronouncement, "You are dust." Man had been made out of dust, but was raised to the apex of all of God's creation. He is now fallen back to where he started. Bear in mind that anyone who remains in Adamic rebellion is also dust, mere dust, but worse than that, dust under judgment and dust to be punished eternally. Painful as these pronouncements were to God, He was compelled by His righteousness to make them. What else could He do?

ADAM, THE STARTING POINT OF THE OLD CREATION

Until Adam sinned, there was no old creation. All was God's one creation. When Adam sinned, he became the starting point the beginning of the old creation. He became the starting point of the old creation through disobedience. Faced with the choice between remaining God's one creation and becoming the starting point of another creation outside of God's will, he decided that he would be the beginning of another creation, and he got what he opted for.

GOD'S IMAGE IN ADAM

God had said in the beginning,

"Let us make man in our image, after our likeness" (Genesis 1:26).

Adam was originally made in the image and likeness of God the Father, the Son and the Holy Spirit. This was God's perfect image. When he sinned, the God-image in him became twisted, bent, crooked, distorted, ruined. It remained God's image, but it was God's image out of shape. It was like a car that had been involved in a terrible accident. It could be recognized as a car, but how different from the original car!

Because the image in man remains God's image though out of shape, fallen man, irrespective of his spiritual condition, can still manifest some virtue, authority and dominion. However, because the image is distorted, the same person who manifests virtue in one area of his character can be utterly wicked in another area. Fallen man is a split personality, capable of much good and much evil.

ALL HUMAN BEINGS ARE PART OF THE OLD CREATION

Had Adam never given birth to anyone, he would have been the only one to be in the old creation, and at his death, the old creation would have ended. However, the Bible says,

> "When Adam had lived a hundred and thirty years, he became the father of a son in his own likeness, after his image" (Genesis 5:3).

Adam's son was, therefore, after Adam's fallen, twisted, and distorted image, and not after the original image which God had made Adam in.

All human beings are descendants of Adam. This means that at birth they enter the world as part of the old creation with a twisted image of God in them. As part of the old creation, all human beings possess a sin-nature at birth. They do not have to commit any particular sin, as Adam did, in order to become sinners. They are sinners at birth. They do not learn to be sinners. They are born sinners.

How can one know if someone is part of the old creation or not? How can one know if a person is a sinner or not? To answer these questions, one needs to ask only one question, "Was he born of parents who descended from Adam?" or "Is he a human being?" If the answer is, "Yes," then that settles it. That person is a sinner - he is part of the old creation and a sinner by nature. If the person were a goat or a stone, he would be exempted. As a sinner, man is separated from God. He is an old creation.

All human beings are born out of God's family! They are born into the devil's kingdom. They are born separated from God and hostile to Him. They possess a nature at birth which is rebellious to the will of God.

Adam was the only one who was born out of the old creation and entered the old creation through a personal act of sin. All other human beings enter the old creation, not by choice, but by BIRTH. There is nothing that anyone can do to ensure that he enters the world but not as part of the old creation. Even the children of believers enter the world as part of the old creation. The faith of their parents does not impart something to them that enables them to be born without a sin-nature. Sin came into the world through the work of Satan. Satan is the originator of the old creation. It is his masterpiece. Having given it origin, he is sustaining it and will bring it to consummation in the lake of fire. He has a kingdom and a destiny.

All human beings are born into the kingdom of Satan. At birth, each child enters the world with the devil as father, and not God. The Lord Jesus said to the religious leaders of His day,

> *"You are of your father the devil, and your will is to do your father's desires. He was a murderer from the beginning, and has nothing to do with the truth, because there is no truth in him. When he lies, he speaks according to his own nature, for he is a liar and the father of lies" (John 8:44).*

All human beings are born as sinners without any exception whatsoever. The Bible says,

> *"The Lord saw that the wickedness of man was great in the earth, and that every imagination of the thoughts of his heart was only evil continually" (Genesis 6:5).*

It further says,

> *"They are corrupt, they do abominable deeds, there is NONE that does good. The Lord looks down from heaven upon the children of men,*

to see if there are any that act wisely, that seek after God. They have ALL gone astray, they are ALL alike corrupt; there is none that does good, no, not one" (Psalm 14:1-3).

"We have ALL become like one who is unclean, and ALL our righteous deeds are like a polluted garment. We ALL fade like a leaf, and our iniquities, like the wind, take us away. There is NO ONE that calls upon thy name" (Isaiah 64:6-7).

"The heart is deceitful above all things, and desperately corrupt; who can understand it?" (Jeremiah 17:9).

"'None is righteous, no, NOT ONE; NO ONE understands, NO ONE seeks for God. ALL have turned aside, together they have gone wrong; no one does good, not even one.' Their throat is an open grave, they use their tongues to deceive" (Romans 3:10-13).

"ALL have sinned and fall short of the glory of God" (Romans 3:23).

The Bible insists that all have sinned. The words ALL and NONE tell us who is involved: everybody! There are no exceptions. A doctor of philosophy and a pupil in Form One are both sinners by nature. A University Professor and the most ignorant jungle-dweller are both sinners. The richest man and the poorest beggar are both sinners. A pastor or priest and a prostitute are both sinners. A black person and a white person are both sinners. The most cultured man living in the heart of Paris, London or New York and the most primitive jungle-dweller in Africa or South America are both sinners.

Education or civilisation does not change the human heart. As far as our sinful nature is concerned, education mainly provides a method of hiding sin and pretending that it is absent. The educated man is a sophisticated sinner. When a primitive man hates you, he immediately tells you so, or the expression on his face tells you. However, the educated man will smile even when hatred boils in his heart. The two hearts are fundamentally the same.

SIN IN PRACTICE

If each sinner had a sin-factory inside him that was permanently out of action and, therefore, produced no sins, the situation would be slightly different. There would arise the temptation to think that the sin-factory was absent. The truth, however, is that the factory of sin in man is working full-time, even though the productivity may vary from person to person.

What are some of the products from the sin-factory inside man? There are some products that may be hidden inside man and are, therefore, not immediately obvious. At the top of the list is independence from God, which is the root sin. God is seen as an interferer. He may be invited by man to render some help in times of sickness or sorrow. He may be asked to go with man to church meetings, ... However, when it comes to the details as to how man spends his money, treats his friends, reacts and relates to the opposite sex, He must keep His distance and not interfere. There are sins committed in the mind like looking at women lustfully:

"Every one who looks at a woman lustfully has already committed adultery with her in his heart" (Matthew 5:28).

Another such sin is hatred. Most people hate one person or the other, yet the Bible says,

"*Any one who hates his brother is a murderer, and you know that no murderer has eternal life abiding in him*" (1 John 3:15).

Then there is the main sin of failing to love God

"*with all your heart, and with all your soul, and with all your strength, and with all your mind; and your neighbour as yourself*" (Luke 10:27).

There are other sins that are downright open. These include:

"All manner of wickedness, evil, covetousness, malice, envy, murder,
strife, deceit, malignity, gossip, slander, hating God, insolence,
haughtiness" (Romans 1:29-31).

"Fornication, impurity, licentiousness, idolatry, sorcery, enmity, strife,
jealousy, anger, selfishness, dissension, party spirit, envy,
drunkenness, carousing" (Galatians 5:19-21).

Broken engagements, broken friendships, broken marriages, broken homes, countless children born outside of wedlock, unfaithful wives/husbands, unfaithful friends, corruption at all levels, nepotism, and so on, all point to the fact that humanity is sin-sick.

These are just a few of the manifestations of sin in practice. The particular manifestations of sin in any life may vary with background, education, circumstances,... but there will always be manifestations of sin in all lives. Some people may be great liars, others given to anger, others to sexual sins, others to pride,... but there will never be any lack of evidence that all human beings practise sin.

No one needs to commit the whole range of sins cited above in order to know that he is a sinner. If you commit one of the above sins, it immediately shows you up for what you are a sinner. The Bible says,

"For whoever keeps the whole law but fail in one point has become
guilty of all of it" (James 2:10).

Look at it in this way. If a mango tree bears ten thousand mangoes, it is a mango tree. On the other hand, if another mango tree bears only ten mangoes, does it cease to be a mango tree because it is less productive? No! It, too, is a mango tree. So the sinner who sins a little and the sinner who sins much are both sinners. They both have one father the devil and they both belong to the old creation. They are both separated from God: lost.

As you read through this catalogue of sins and sinful attitudes, and as you look into your heart and life, do you agree with God's Word that you as an individual are a sinner and that you fall short of the glory of God? If you have never committed even one sin, then, God's Word has lied and you are free, and the rest of this book is not for you!

THE WAGES OF SIN

Adam's sin resulted in separation between him and God. This is death. Death was Adam's salary for sinning. Death remains the salary for sin. The Bible says, *"The wages of sin is death"* (Romans 6:23). A holy God cannot tolerate sin. He must punish sin. Putting it in other words, He must give the sinner a salary for sinning. Let me illustrate this with a true story. Some years ago, while I was a Lecturer at Makerere University, Kampala, a certain Professor whose name I prefer to call Dr. X and myself went to the University bank at the end of the month to inquire into the state of our finances. We both asked for our bank balances, but he soon found out that no money had been credited to his account that month. His salary had not been paid in. He became even more furious when he found out that I had my own salary paid in. He fumed in anger, saying aloud, "I have worked for this nonsense University for the whole month, and here I am without a salary." He paced the floor of the bank up and down as he spoke aloud. He was no longer the calm, well-behaved academician whom we all knew him to be. He had the right to be angry. He had worked, but failed to receive his salary. It was not fair to him. Although the University made a mistake about his salary, God will make no such mistake. He is above mistakes. He will give each sinner his fully earned salary. You, sinner, will receive your pay.

THE NATURE OF SIN'S SALARY

Sin's salary is twofold. First of all, there is the salary advance, and afterwards, there will be the full pay.

Salary advance:

When a person is employed in our national civil service, he is given some portion of his pay as salary advance. This enables him to live. It is not his full pay, but it guarantees the fact that the full pay will come in time. There is also a salary advance for sin. It includes heartbreaks, broken relationships, venereal diseases that result in sterility, abortions, unwanted pregnancies, unwed mothers, prostitution, criminals who are imprisoned, mental diseases resulting from psychological disorders, poverty resulting from drunkenness, accidents caused by drunken drivers, and so on. The failure of man to realise his full potential because of sin is alarming. Think of the growing rate of divorce, suicide, and so on. Think of the homes that are broken by quarrels or the wrong use of family resources. Think of the suffering of the poor because the rich hoard all the money. Think of the suffering that is caused to many when the wrong person occupies a post he does not deserve because of favouritism or bribery. These are the first instalments of the salary that sin earns.

Full pay:

When someone who has been on salary advance has undergone the necessary medical examination and had his certificates carefully checked, he is integrated into our national civil service. He then begins to earn his full pay and has his arrears paid to him as well as rent and family allowances. Often it takes time, but the government ensures that in the end everyone earns all his salary right to the last franc.

The sinner who continues in his sin will face God's final judgment, be sentenced and integrated into the devil's civil service called hell. The Bible says,

> "*It is appointed for men to die once, and after that comes judgment*"
> (Hebrews 9:27).

In preparation for the Judgment Day, God is keeping a record of every man's actions. All sins that are committed in thought, word and deed by you are being faithfully recorded against your name in the heavenly record. It is as if a second by second filming and recording of your thoughts, words and deeds is continuously in progress. Your life is being filmed. The film of your life will be projected on the Judgment Day for you and every other person to see. The things done in darkness will then be shown in the light. Nothing is being left out in the daily record of your actions, words and thoughts, and nothing will be left out unprojected for you and for others to see. Sentence means that sinners shall be sent away from God's presence to everlasting hell.

> *"Do you not know that the unrighteous will not inherit the kingdom of God? Do not be deceived; neither fornicators, nor idolaters, nor adulterers, nor homosexuals, nor thieves, nor the greedy, nor drunkards, nor revilers, nor robbers will inherit the kingdom of God"* (1 Corinthians 6:9-10).

> *"But as for the cowardly, the faithless, the polluted, as for the murderers, fornicators, sorcerers, idolaters, and all liars, their lot shall be in the lake that burns with fire and sulphur, which is the second death"* (Revelation 21:8).

The Judgment Day will be pay day. Jesus Christ will be the Chief Judge. The Bible says,

> *"The Father judges no one, but has given all judgment to the Son"* (John 5:22).

Jesus' words of sentence to unrepentant sinners will be:

> *"Depart from me, you cursed, into the eternal fire prepared for the devil and his angels"* (Matthew 25:41).

These words of judgment will take immediate effect, for the Bible says,

> *"And they will go away into eternal punishment"* (Matthew 25:46).

The eternal punishment will be in the lake of fire called hell. Hell is also called

"*Everlasting fire*" (Matthew 25:41),

"*Eternal punishment*" (Matthew 25:46),

"*Outer darkness*" (Matthew 8:12).

It is the lake that burns with sulphur (Revelation 21:8). It is the second death (Revelation 21:8).

THE END OF THE OLD CREATION

The devil who is the originator of the old creation will be destroyed. The Bible says,

> "*And the devil who had deceived them was thrown into the lake of fire and sulphur where the beast and the false prophet were, and they will be tormented day and night for ever and ever*" (Revelation 20:10).

Hades and Death were also cast into hell. The Bible says,

> "*And the sea gave up the dead in it, Death and Hades gave up the dead in them, and all were judged by what they had done. Then Death and Hades were thrown into the lake of fire. This is the second death, the lake of fire; and if any one's name was not found written in the book of life, he was thrown into the lake of fire*" (Revelation 20:13-15).

TO THE READER

Dear Reader,

What all this means is that you, whether you believe it or not, are separated from God and hell-bound, unless you have taken or do now take the right steps to remedy the situation. Hell is your salary for sin, and God will faithfully ensure that you have your rightly deserved pay. This is very fair. God must punish sin, or else He would contradict Himself. Does that matter to you? Will you do something about it?

QUESTIONS: (SUPPORT YOUR ANSWERS WITH BIBLE VERSES)

1. How did God see man and the rest of His creation from the beginning?
2. Show clearly that you understand the reasons why God created man.
3. What two trees were there in the centre of the garden?
4. Did God permit that Adam and Eve should eat the fruits of all the trees in the garden?
5. Which tree were they not supposed to eat the fruits of and why?
6. Did Adam obey?
7. What is sin and what are sins?
8. Have you ever sinned?
9. In what ways have you sinned?
10. What were the immediate consequences of Adam's sin?
11. God had said that Adam would die on the day that he ate of the fruit of the forbidden tree. Did Adam die the day he ate the fruit?
12. What is: (a) physical death? (b) spiritual death?
13. How did Adam's sin affect the purpose for which he was created?
14. What happened to the image of God in Adam after he sinned?
15. How did Adam become the starting point of the old creation?
16. How does one become part of the old creation?
17. Into what kingdom are all human beings born? Whom do all human beings have as their father at birth?
18. Who is your father?
19. Which human being has never sinned? Name some such people whom you know have never sinned.
20. Must God reward sinners for their sin?

21. What are some of the immediate consequences of sin that you have experienced in your own life or seen in the lives of people that you know?
22. What will be the final salary for sin?
23. Is there any reason to hope that you will not be paid the final salary for your sin?

2

HUMAN ATTEMPTS AT GETTING OUT OF THE OLD CREATION

W hen Adam sinned, God sent him out of the garden of Eden. He was driven out by the Lord. In order to ensure that the return of man on his (man's) initiative and conditions was rendered unsuccessful, God

"placed the cherubim, and a flaming sword which turned every way, to guard the way to the tree of life" (Genesis 3:24).

God has never intended that anyone who has become a part of the old creation should return to Him on his (man's) own terms and by his own effort. All such attempts infuriate God. They are a part of man's rebellion. The way back must be initiated by God. Man, in his rebellion, has tried on his own to get back to God, but it has always been a failure. We shall look at some of the attempts of man to get back to God.

ISLAM, BUDDHISM, BAHAI FAITH, ...

These are all moral religions. They teach that man should live a good life and be rightly related to God. They have laws or commandments which man cannot keep. There is no Saviour and no Cross. Man is his own saviour.

HEATHENISM, AFRICAN RELIGIONS, WHITE MAGIC AND ALL THE RELIGIONS OF PAGANS

In these, there is no true knowledge of the Saviour or His Cross, but there is true knowledge of evil powers, which man tries to appease by offering sacrifices to them because man has proved their existence. God is out of reach and may be contacted through mediums, ancestors, etc.

HUMANISM

It is the religion of those who have raised man to the level of God. They have rejected God and His laws, and given His place to man. Communism and all the religions of those who call themselves "Free thinkers" are included in this group.

IMPOTENT CHRISTIANITY

This is a form of religion that bears the name of Jesus Christ, but knows nothing of His power to save sinners. Here the name Jesus is mentioned. His cross is mentioned, but He has no pre-eminent place. He is mentioned and sometimes worshipped, but not as the Lord. The adherents live as if Jesus never died to save sinners from sin and were not coming back to judge the world. We shall look at each of these inventions of man and see why they cannot bring anyone out of the old creation.

THE FAILURE OF MORAL RELIGIONS

The fundamental basis of moral religions is this: man is fundamentally good. He sins by error. When he sins he displeases God, who will punish him for his failure. If he can try hard, God will weigh his good and his evil. Depending on the quantity and perhaps quality of his actions, God will decide whether or not he is to suffer in the life after death or to have life with Him. So in Islam, man tries by many prayers, alms to the poor, fasting, trips to Mecca, and so on, to make up a credit balance in which the good outweighs the evil. He hopes that by this he will be acceptable to God.

First of all, let me say that because of these attempts to please God, some people, who are truly committed in moral religions like Islam, are fine people. They are kind and helpful, since they hope to gain heaven by that way. However, there is a fundamental problem. We have seen that man is a sinner - a lost sinner. He cannot get back to God on his own. Even if he committed only one sin, he would still be lost. Man cannot save himself. Man's attempts are futile, because the Bible says,

> *"We have all become like one who is unclean, and all our righteous deeds are like a polluted garment"* (Isaiah 64:6).

Yes, all the good deeds of a moralist are like a polluted garment before God. They may be good before man, but they are useless before God. Another failure of moral religions is this: they do not provide a way of dealing with past sins. Even if a thief were capable of stopping and stealing no more, he would still be accountable for his past thefts!

Because moral religions are fundamentally man's attempts at reaching God, because fundamentally God is unknown and unapproachable, all people in these religions have no assurance of forgiveness of sins. It is right that they should have no assurance of forgiveness, since they are not forgiven. What happens to their many prayers? Well, as sinners the prayers leave their lips, bounce on the wall of sin that separates them from God, and returns to them. Their prayers do not reach God. Someone may ask, "What of their sincerity?" Well, true. They are sincere. They are sincere, but sincerity is not enough. They are sincerely mistaken. They are sincere, but lost. If a man sincerely believes a lie, will his sincerity change the lie into the truth? No!

The moral religionist must look for a way back to God. Only God can provide one, and He has provided one in the death, resurrection, and glorification of the Lord Jesus.

THE FAILURE OF PAGAN RELIGIONS

Pagans are found all over the world. They are found in Paris, London, New York, Africa, Asia and other parts of the world. Paganism is not the primitive man's religion as some would have us believe. Paganism includes all forms of magic, sorcery, witchcraft, astrology, ancestral worship, and so on. The fundamentals of paganism are gods who must be appeased by sacrifices. The reality of the unseen realm is known, and man wants to appease the gods. So there is propitiation (blood sacrifices to the gods), or there is libation (drink offerings to the gods). By various forms of libation and magic practices, man tries to know the mind of the gods in order to appease them. Man also wants to please the gods in order to have favours from them. Paganism knows and worships many gods, even where these gods are seen as representing the supreme God.

In a lot of pagan religions, the supreme God is seen as so holy and so totally unapproachable that He can only be contacted through mediums: human beings who act as intermediaries. Other human beings function as priests, witches, wizards, ...

Pagans worship idols who are meant to represent God. All this is useless in bringing man out of the old creation. It is also direct disobedience to God who said,

"You shall have no other gods besides me" (Exodus 20:3);

and

"You shall not make for yourself a graven image, or any likeness of anything that is in heaven above, or that is in the earth beneath or that is in the water under the earth; you shall not bow down to them or serve them; for I the Lord your God am a jealous God" (Exodus 20:4-5).

The whole of paganism is so much against God that the Lord said,

"There shall not be found among you any one who burns his son or his

daughter as an offering, any one who practises divination, a soothsayer, or an augur, or a sorcerer, or a charmer, or a medium, or a wizard, or a necromancer. For whoever does these things is an abomination to the Lord" (Deuteronomy 18:10-12).

The Word of the Lord says,

"The idols of the nations are silver and gold, the work of men's hands. They have mouths, but they speak not, they have eyes, but they see not, they have ears, but they hear not, nor is there any breath in their mouths. LIKE THEM BE THOSE WHO MAKE THEM! YEA, EVERY ONE WHO TRUSTS IN THEM!" (Psalm 135:15-18).

All who practise paganism are lost. The sacrifices that they offer are not to the true God, but to demons. The Bible says,

"What do I imply then? That food offered to idols is anything, or that an idol is anything? No, I imply that what pagans sacrifice they offer to demons and not to God" (1 Corinthians 10:19-20).

Their ancestors are not intermediaries between them and the true God; rather demons act as ancestors and unite them with the unseen world of Satan.

Paganism cannot bring anyone out of the old creation. It can only plunge people deeper and deeper into perdition. What of pagans who practise paganism out of ignorance? What if they are sincere? Well, sincerity is not enough. No one is set free even before an earthly court for not knowing what the law says. All sorcerers and pagans of all forms will have their part in the lake which burns with fire and sulphur. The way out is through repentance and faith in the Lord Jesus, who is God's one Way of salvation.

THE FAILURE OF HUMANISM, COMMUNISM, AND SO ON

Humanism and communism are religions. They are the religions of faith in man. They say,

 We do not need God. We can do without Him. God has never existed or, even if He existed, He must have died.

First of all, it requires supreme knowledge to be able to say that there is no God. Think with me for a moment. Of all the knowledge of Science in all its ramifications, knowledge of the humanities, and so on, knowledge of the billions of stars that there are and of all the seas and all that they contain, do you think that you have 5% of the total knowledge that there is in the entire universe? To make such a claim is already being presumptuous. However, even if you possessed such knowledge (say about 5%), how can you say that God does not exist in what you do not know? I well remember a colleague who said that he possessed less than 0. 1% of all that can be known, but also said that he was sure that in the 99.9% of the knowledge that he did not have, God did not exist. How ridiculous! He knew that God did not exist in what he did not know!

No intelligent person can say that God does not exist. To say so is to claim total knowledge. The least thing that an intelligent person should say is that he does not know if there is God. However, it is not enough to remain ignorant. Any intelligent person should actively find out if there is God, and should not rest until he has found Him.

Humanism believes in man, but when you look around and see the fragility and weakness of man, you are forced to confess that the deification of man is absolute folly.

What if a person does not believe that there is God? What if he is a "Free thinker without any commitments"? Well, he must remain part of the old creation and face God some day. When he will be languishing in the lake of fire, he will be a true believer in God then, but it will be too late.

THE FAILURE OF IMPOTENT CHRISTIANITY, THE INSUFFICIENT CROSS

Normally, true Christianity is God's unquestionable answer to the whole business of man's perdition. However, religious men have been tricked by the Enemy and, in response to his activities, they have put forward something that is very far removed from that which is true and of God. They have done this by their attitude to the Word of God, either in part or in whole:

1. putting the Word of God entirely aside,
2. adding to Scripture the thoughts of men,
3. distorting the teaching of Scripture,
4. weakening the authority of Scripture.

The ultimate aim of the Enemy is to hide, distort or put aside the revelation of God concerning the Cross of Calvary, where Satan was overthrown by Jesus and freedom obtained for all his captives. Impotent Christianity ensures that the devil holds sway over the souls of men. For example, many who call themselves Christians are idol-worshippers. They bow to statues and worship human beings called saints, and believe in salvation by faith plus good works, yet the Bible says,

> *"You shall not make for yourself a graven image, or any likeness of anything that is in heaven above, or that is in the earth beneath or that is in the water under the earth; you shall not bow down to them or serve them"* (Exodus 20: 4-5).

Sunday by Sunday, multitudes of religious people bow down to statues and pray through human beings, instead of praying in the name of Jesus. They have multitudes of mediators in addition to Jesus. All this they do in full knowledge of the fact that the Word of God says,

> *"For there is one God, and there is one mediator between God and*
> *men, the man Christ Jesus, who gave himself as a ransom for all,*
> *the testimony to which was borne at the proper time"* (1 Timothy
> 2:5-6).

The Word of God is far from central. In an attempt to amass numbers into the religious systems, and not into Christ, multitudes of babies and adults are sprinkled and deceived that they are believers, even though they have neither repented nor believed personally in Christ. All this is done in full knowledge of the fact that the Lord Jesus said,

> *"He who believes and is baptized will be saved"* (Mark 16:16).

The product is entire nations of baptized, confirmed sinners twice more fit for hell than a pagan who has never passed by the walls of a religious meeting place.

If you are trusting in some religious system to get you out of the old creation, you will end up in hell. It does not matter the name of the religious system. It will not save. It cannot save.

What of those who believe in salvation through Jesus plus good works? All these, too, are lost, because the good works that an unbeliever performs in the hope that they will gain him a standing before God, are actually dead works. An unbeliever is considered by the Lord as dead. The Bible says that those who are not rightly related to the Lord Jesus are dead. In talking of the past life of the Ephesian believers, the apostle said,

> *"And you he made alive, when you were dead through the trespasses*
> *and sins in which you once walked"* (Ephesians 2:1-2).

A sinner is dead in his sins. All that a dead person produces is dead. The good works of a sinner are dead works. When he believes, he should repent of having committed the sin of counting on good works for salvation. The Bible says,

"Therefore let us leave the elementary doctrine of Christ and go on to maturity, not laying again a foundation of repentance from dead works and of faith toward God" (Hebrews 6:1).

If an unbeliever gives money for God's work, he commits a sin. If he prays (except the prayer of repentance towards God and faith in the Lord Jesus) his prayer is sin. If he does good acts, they are acts of sin, for all that issues from an unbeliever bears the marks of the unbeliever's father the devil. The Lord Jesus told the religious leaders of His day,

"You are of your father the devil ..." (John 8:44).

In impotent Christianity (impotent because it cannot save) there is an inadequate Christ and an inadequate Cross. So people depend on Christ plus good works for salvation. The Bible says,

"For by grace you have been saved through faith; and this is not your own doing, it is the gift of God not because of works, lest any man should boast" (Ephesians 2:8-9).

Of course, all saved people will do good works, but these good works will never add anything to their salvation, for, from the moment that a person repents towards God and receives the Lord Jesus, he receives one hundred per cent justification from God. He can never add anything to it.

Because of the whole distortion of these systems that have an inadequate Saviour, sinners are not brought face to face with the Lord Jesus who saves to the uttermost those who believe in Him. Because of this inadequacy, numerous things must be done by the people to add to their inadequate faith, and the product is a multitude of baptized, confirmed, and sincere men and women on their way to hell.

The attempt to get back to God by good works is saying to God, "Although You say that I am altogether wrong, I want to prove to You that You do not quite know what You are talking about, for, see how good I am!"

Salvation by faith plus good works is the devil's creation aimed at blinding people from seeing God's way of salvation. This may offend you, but God says,

> *"For my thoughts are not your thoughts, neither are your ways my*
> *ways, says the Lord. For as the heavens are higher than the earth,*
> *so are my ways higher than your ways and my thoughts than your*
> *thoughts" (Isaiah 55:8-9).*

Some honest people think that they can be saved by keeping the law. We know that God gave the law of nature to the non-Jews. The Bible says,

> *"For what can be known about God is plain to them, because God has*
> *shown it to them. Ever since the creation of the world his invisible*
> *nature, namely, his eternal power and deity, has been clearly*
> *perceived in the things that have been made. So they are without*
> *excuse" (Romans 1:19-20).*

> *"When Gentiles who have not the law do by nature what the law*
> *requires, they are a law to themselves, even though they do not*
> *have the law. They show that what the law requires is written on*
> *their hearts, while their conscience also bears witness and their*
> *conflicting thoughts accuse or perhaps excuse them on that day*
> *when, according to my gospel, God judges the secrets of men by*
> *Christ Jesus" (Romans 2:14-16).*

God also gave the law called the ten commandments to the Jews.

To be candid, God knew that although the law was perfect and faultless, man would never keep it. The law was given so that it might serve as a mirror of how sinful man was, and thus when a man saw his sinfulness revealed by the law, he would fly to God's only true provision for sin - the blood of Christ. The Bible says,

> *"For all who rely on works of the law are under a curse; for it is*
> *written, 'Cursed be every one who does not abide by all things*
> *written in the book of the law, and do them.' Now it is evident*
> *that no man is justified before God by the law" (Galatians*
> *3:10-11).*

> *"For whoever keeps the whole law but fail IN ONE POINT has*
> *become guilty of all of it" (James 2:10).*

Nothing could be more frustrating to anyone who wants to become a new creation and he attempts to accomplish this by keeping the law. The Bible further says,

> *"Now we know that whatever the law says it speaks to those who are*
> *under the law, so that every mouth may be stopped, and the whole*
> *world may be held accountable to God. FOR NO HUMAN*
> *BEING WILL BE JUSTIFIED (PUT INTO RIGHT*
> *STANDING) IN HIS (GOD'S) SIGHT BY WORKS OF*
> *THE LAW, SINCE THROUGH THE LAW COMES*
> *KNOWLEDGE OF SIN" (Romans 3:19-20).*

The law is good, but man is weak and sold under sin. If he could keep the law perfectly and not fail in any point of it, he would not need a Saviour. He would be his own saviour. Unfortunately, no one has ever kept the law perfectly. So all men need a Saviour. All men need the Saviour.

It is not enough to belong to some denominational system, to be baptized and confirmed. If an unrepentant sinner is baptized, the product is a baptized, confirmed sinner, twice as fit for hell than the pagan!

Why can human attempts not save man? Why can they not change him into a new creation? The answer lies fundamentally in the nature of sin. Sin renders the sinner dead. If you tell a dead man not to decay, he will decay all the same. If you clothe him with expensive clothes, he will still decay.

Even if you inject formalin into him to prevent him from decaying, he will still decay. Even if he did not want to decay, he would decay all the same because the law of death and decay is at work in him.

The various religions are like the good clothes which are put on the corpse or the formalin injected into it, but all that is produced is a well-dressed corpse. What the dead man needs is not the law. He does not need a preservative. He does not need good clothes. He needs life.

Give it life and later on its clothing can be taken care of. That is God's way of handling the problem, and He did it by the death and resurrection of the Lord Jesus. In the next lesson we shall look at that more closely, but let us state categorically that Jesus is God's way back to life. He said,

> *"The thief comes only to steal and kill and destroy; I came that they may have life, and have it abundantly"* (John 10: 10).

He further said,

> *"And this is eternal life, that they know thee the only true God, and Jesus Christ whom thou hast sent"* (John 17:3).

John the apostle said,

> *"And this is the testimony, that God gave us eternal life, and this life is in his Son. He who has the Son has life; he who has not the Son of God has not life"* (1 John 5:11-12).

May I ask you a personal question? It is this: "Do you have the Son of God resident in you?" If yes, you have life. If not, you are a corpse.

QUESTIONS

1. What did God do to ensure that fallen man could not return to Him on his (man's) own condition?

2. What is the fundamental basis of moral religions?
3. Why can moral religions not save man?
4. Can a sincere man perish? If yes, why?
5. What is idolatry? What power do sorcerers use?
6. How does God regard the idol and the idol-worshipper?
7. Does it matter if a person does not believe in God?
8. If someone believes a lie but believes it very sincerely, will God not pardon him on the basis of his faith and ignore the fact that his faith is based on a lie?
9. In what ways does the devil attempt to destroy the truth of God's Word?
10. What is wrong with idolatry that is carried out in the name of Christ?
11. Can baptism and confirmation carried out by some religious system in the name of Christ save the person?
12. Why can no one be saved by keeping the law?
13. What is wrong with salvation by faith and good works?
14. Which is the way of salvation?
15. Do you want to be saved now?

3

GOD'S WAY OUT OF THE OLD CREATION

We have seen very clearly that man is lost. He is considered by God as dead. He is a helpless corpse that cannot help itself in a way that meets its needs and satisfies the heart of God. All his attempts at getting out of the old creation are futile. They are resisted by God and rendered useless before Him.

If there is to be a way out of the old life, it must come through the initiative of God. Initially, it was God who sent sinful man away. He is the One whose heart was broken by the rebellion of man. The law that the sinner broke was God's. Only God knows best what must be done to re-establish peace between Him and the sinner, get the sinner out of the old creation, and make him a part of the new creation.

THE SHEDDING OF BLOOD

Even in the garden, before man was expelled from it, the first shedding of blood on behalf of man took place. God saw the exposed nakedness of Adam and Eve, and had compassion on them. He saw the fact that the leaves that they had used to cover their nakedness were not sufficient to cover them. Out of His love for them, love that went out from Him unto them even in their sinful condition, He made garments of skin for them (Genesis 3:21). In order to have this skin, He shed the blood of animals. He was sort of ordaining the shedding of blood as the one way of meeting man's need that would satisfy Him (GOD). He knew that man's problem was deeper than physical nakedness. He thus ordained that by the means of the shedding of blood, man's deepest need, which is reconciliation to Him, would be met, and not by human works.

THE BLOOD AND THE CHILDREN OF ISRAEL IN EGYPT

When God decided to deliver the children of Israel out of the bondage of Egypt and bring judgment on the gods of Egypt, the Egyptian king and his people, He used blood to grant safety to the children of Israel. He told the children of Israel to take a lamb without blemish, kill it, take some of its blood and put it on the two door posts and the lintel of the houses (Exodus 12:3, 5, 7). He further said,

> "*For I will pass through the land of Egypt that night, and I will smite all the first-born in the land of Egypt, both man and beast; and on all the gods of Egypt I will execute judgment: I am the Lord. THE BLOOD SHALL BE A SIGN FOR YOU, UPON THE HOUSES WHERE YOU ARE; AND WHEN I SEE THE BLOOD, I WILL PASS OVER YOU, AND NO PLAGUE SHALL FALL UPON YOU TO DESTROY YOU, WHEN I SMITE THE LAND OF EGYPT*" (Exodus 12:12-13).

This rite was called,

> "*The sacrifice of the Lord's passover*" (Exodus 12:27).

The angel was to pass through the land of Egypt and he would pass over any house that was marked with blood. The children of Israel obeyed. God kept His word. The angel passed through the land of Egypt destroying all the first-born. He also passed over all the houses of Israel which were marked with blood.

Why were the children of Israel spared? It was not because they were more righteous than the Egyptians. It was not because they sought God more diligently than the Egyptians. They were spared because the destroyer saw the blood; for God had said, "When I see the blood, I will pass over you."

Why were the Egyptians destroyed? It was not because they had sinned more. It was because they did not have the mark of blood. The Egyptian first-born were all destroyed. Even "good" Egyptian first-born were smitten by the angel. The criterion for being spared that night was not human goodness. It was the presence of blood on the door posts. Indeed,

> *"Without the shedding of blood there is no forgiveness of sins"*
> (Hebrews 9:22).

JESUS CHRIST - GOD'S PASSOVER LAMB

As we have seen, there had to be a Passover lamb slain, and its blood applied to the door posts. This lamb was no ordinary one. It had to meet specific requirements. It had to be a lamb

> *"without blemish, a male a year old"* (Exodus 12:5).

When God decided to bring the fallen human race out of the bondage of sin into His new life, He needed a Paschal Lamb without blemish. No human being could fulfil that function, for all have sinned and are, therefore, with blemish. No angel could fulfil the role; for angels are really not human beings.

Jesus Christ alone could fulfil that role; for He was truly human, born of a woman, and born under the law. The Bible says,

> *"But when the time had fully come, God sent forth his Son, born of woman, born under the law, to redeem those who were under the law, so that we might receive adoption as sons"* (Galatians 4:4-5).

Jesus was also without blemish. He was without sin. The Bible says,

> *"For we have not a high priest who is unable to sympathize with our weaknesses, but one who in every respect has been tempted as we are, yet without sin" (Hebrews 4:15).*

> *"For it was fitting that we should have such a high priest, holy, blameless, unstained, separated from sinners, exalted above the heavens" (Hebrews 7:26).*

> *"For to this you have been called, because Christ also suffered for you, leaving you an example, that you should follow in his steps. He committed no sin; no guile was found on his lips. When he was reviled, he did not revile in return; when he suffered, he did not threaten; but he trusted to him who judges justly" (I Peter 2:21-23).*

Jesus came to this world to be God's Paschal Lamb. John the Baptist said of Him,

> *"Behold, the Lamb of God!"* (John 1:36).

The Lamb of God is Jesus' greatest title. Even in the Kingdom of God when all that has to do with sin will have been settled and finished with eternally, the Lord Jesus will continue to bear His great title, "Lamb." The Bible says,

> *"Then he showed me the river of the water of life, bright as crystal, flowing from the throne of God and of the Lamb ... There shall no more be anything accursed, but the throne of God and of the Lamb shall be in it, and his servants shall worship him"* (Revelation 22:1-3).

JESUS CHRIST - GOD'S LAMB - BORN TO DIE

A lamb has ultimately only one destiny - death. Even before the Lord of all Glory came on earth, He knew that He had only one destiny on earth - death. He said,

> "For the Son of man also came not to be served but to serve, and to give his life as a ransom for many" (Mark 10:45).

He did not die by accident, nor was death forced upon Him. Long before He went to the cross, He said,

> "I lay down my life, that I may take it again. No one takes it from me, but I lay it down of my own accord. I have power to lay it down, and I have power to take it again; this charge I have received from my Father" (John 10:17-19).

Jesus - born to die! He persistently talked about His death. The Bible says,

> "And he began to teach them that the Son of man must suffer many things, and be rejected by the elders and the chief priests and the scribes, and be killed, and after three days rise again" (Mark 8:31).

Again He said to them,

> "The Son of man will be delivered into the hands of men, and they will kill him; and when he is killed, after three days he will rise" (Mark 9:31).

He further said,

> "Behold, we are going up to Jerusalem; and the Son of man will be delivered to the chief priests and the scribes, and they will condemn him to death, and deliver him to the Gentiles; and they will mock him, and spit upon him, and scourge him, and kill him; and after three days he will rise" (Mark 10:33-34).

Jesus was not only born to die. He was crucified, and competent authority affirmed the fact that He was dead.

WHY DID JESUS DIE?

1. Jesus died as a manifestation of God's love for a lost world. The Bible says, "For God so loved the world that he gave his only Son, that whoever believes in him should not perish but have eternal life" (John 3:16). *"But God shows his love for us in that while we were yet sinners Christ died for us"* (Romans 5:8). *"In this the love of God was made manifest among us, that God sent his only Son into the world, so that we might live through him"* (1 John 4:9).

2. Jesus died to provide the Passover blood. He shed His blood for sinners. He said, *"This is my blood of the new covenant, which is poured out for many for the forgiveness of sins"* (Matthew 26:28). When a sinner comes to Christ, he is covered by the blood of Christ, and God passes over him, even though he has sinned.

3. *He died to mediate a new covenant. The Bible says, "Therefore he is the mediator of a new covenant, so that those who are called may receive the promised eternal inheritance, since a death has occurred which redeems them from the transgressions under the first covenant" (Hebrews 9:15).*

4. He died in order to destroy the film of human sin. As we said earlier, God is filming each human life in preparation for the Judgment Day. In order that there may be hope for the sinner, that film must be destroyed. When Jesus went to the cross He took the film of each life with Him and, there on the cross, He destroyed it. The Word of God says, *"And you, who were dead in trespasses and the uncircumcision of your flesh, God made alive together with him, having forgiven us all our trespasses, having cancelled the bond which stood against us with its legal demands; this he set aside, nailing it to the cross"* (Colossians 2:13-14).

THE DEAD MAN DIED

We have said earlier on that all sinners are dead in trespasses and sins. We have also said that all human beings become part of the old creation through birth. How can the sinner get out of the old creation into which he is born? The answer is that he can get out of the old creation only through death. When Jesus died on the cross, He took with Him all human beings in the old creation, and when he died there they all died with Him. By being united with Him in His death, the dead man died and thus found a way out of the old creation. God's way out of the old creation is through the union of the sinner with Christ in His death on the cross. The sinner dies with Christ on the cross and thus obtains his exit out of the old creation.

THE DEATH OF CHRIST AND SALVATION

Salvation from sin can best be understood in three aspects:

1. Salvation from the consequences of sin.
2. Salvation from the power of sin.
3. Salvation from the presence of sin.

The death of Christ on the cross purchased the salvation of all human beings from the consequence of sin, which is the lake of fire. The Bible says,

> "All we like sheep have gone astray; we have turned every one to his own way; and the Lord has laid on him the iniquity of us all" (Isaiah 53:6).

> "Since, therefore, we are now justified by his blood, much more shall we be saved by him from the wrath of God. For if while we were enemies we were reconciled to God by the death of his Son, much more, now that we are reconciled, shall we be saved by his life" (Romans 5:9-10).

From the moment when a sinner repents and receives Jesus Christ, he is saved from the consequences of sin.

The death of Christ on the cross provides the way for salvation from the power of sin day by day. The Bible says,

> "*We know that our old self was crucified with Him so that the sinful body might be destroyed, and we might no longer be enslaved to sin*" (Romans 6:6).

> "*Those who have died with him are freed from sin*" (Romans 6:7).

All who know Christ know the way to continuous victory over the power of sin day by day. This is wonderful!

Because of the death of Christ on the cross, the believer will be saved from the presence of sin. Those who are already saved from the consequence of sin and who are being saved from the power of sin, nevertheless, live in a sinful world. This will, however, not continue to be the case endlessly. The day is coming when the Lord Jesus will come and take His own away, and they will then be saved from the presence of sin. There in His immediate presence, the Bible says,

> "*We ourselves, who have the first fruits of the Spirit, groan inwardly as we wait for adoption as sons, the redemption of our bodies*" (Romans 8:23).

> "*There shall no more be anything accursed, but the throne of God*" (Revelation 22:3).

THE DEATH OF CHRIST AND THE LAW

As we saw before, man could not keep the law. He would try and fail. The law stood against him. By His death on the cross, the Lord Jesus fulfilled the demands of the law. First of all, the Lord Jesus made the law obsolete. The Bible says,

> "*Now before faith came, we were confined under the law, kept under*

restraint until faith should be revealed. So that the law was our custodian until Christ came, that we might be justified by faith. But now that faith has come, we are no longer under a custodian; for in Christ Jesus you are all sons of God, through faith" (Galatians 3:23-26).

He made the law obsolete by taking it with Him to the cross and bringing it to an end. The Bible says,

"And you, who were dead in trespasses and the uncircumcision of your flesh, God made alive together with him, having forgiven us all our trespasses, having cancelled the bond which stood against us with its legal demands; this he set aside, nailing it to the cross" (Colossians 2:13-14).

The Bible says,

"Cursed be every one who does not abide by all things written in the book of the law, and do them" (Galatians 3:10).

We were under a curse. When Christ went to the cross, He took our curse upon Himself and, as He hung there, He redeemed us from the curse of the law. The Bible says,

"Christ redeemed us from the curse of the law, having become a curse for us" (Galatians 3:13).

Because we have been redeemed from the law, we are no longer under its legal demands for our salvation. We are saved one hundred per cent apart from keeping the law. Glory be to the Lord!

THE DEATH OF CHRIST & BLOOD SACRIFICES

There was the sacrificial system in the Old Testament that was accepted by the Lord for some time. The Bible says,

"Hence even the first covenant was not ratified without blood.

> For when every commandment of the law had been declared by Moses to all the people, he took the blood of calves and goats, with water and scarlet wool and hyssop, and sprinkled both the book itself and all the people, saying, *'This is the blood of the covenant which God commanded you.' And in the same way he sprinkled with the blood both the tent and all the vessels used in worship. Indeed, under the law almost everything is purified with the blood, and without the shedding of blood there is no forgiveness of sins"* (Hebrews 9:18-22).

These sacrifices were inadequate. They could not take away sin. The Bible says,

> *"But in these sacrifices there is a reminder of sin year after year. For it is impossible that the blood of bulls and goats should take away sins" (Hebrews 10:3-4).*

The inadequacy of these sacrifices made the death of Christ necessary. The Bible says,

> *"Consequently, when Christ came into the world, he said, 'Sacrifices and offerings thou hast not desired, but a body thou hast prepared for me; in burnt offerings and sin offerings thou hast taken not pleasure . . .' then he added, 'Lo, I have come to do thy will...'And by that will we have been sanctified through the offering of the body of Jesus Christ ONCE FOR ALL" (Hebrews 10:5-10).*

The sacrifice of Christ was final. The Bible says,

> *"He has appeared once for all at the end of the age to put away sin by the sacrifice of himself" (Hebrews 9:26).*

> *"But when Christ appeared as a high priest of the good things that have come, then through the greater and more perfect tent (not made with hands, that is, not of this creation) he entered ONCE FOR ALL into the Holy place, taking not the blood of goats and*

> *calves but his own blood, thus securing an eternal redemption. For if the sprinkling of defiled persons with the blood of goats and bulls and with the ashes of a heifer sanctifies for the purification of the flesh, how much more shall the blood of Christ, who through the eternal Spirit offered himself without blemish to God, purify your consciences from dead works to serve the living God" (Hebrews 9:11-14).*

Before Jesus offered Himself on the cross as the one sacrifice for sin, other sacrificial systems could be tolerated. By His death, He offered one sacrifice, once and for all. This sacrifice put an end to all the other sacrificial systems.

ABOMINABLE SACRIFICES

From the day that the Lord Jesus died on the cross as God's supreme sacrifice for sin, it is an absolute abomination to offer animal or human sacrifices to God. Such offerings infuriate God enormously and bring God's fullest wrath on the one offering the sacrifice. To keep on offering sacrifices is to reject God's one sacrifice and bear the consequences for that.

THE DEATH OF CHRIST AND THE SATANIC TRINITY

Satan did set up a trinity with which to oppose the Lord. The satanic trinity is an imitation and a counterfeit of God's Trinity. In the satanic trinity there is the devil, the world, and the flesh. The world opposes God the Father. The Bible says,

> *"Do not love the world or the things in the world. If any one loves the world, love for the Father is not in him. For all that is in the world, the lust of the flesh and the lust of the eyes and the pride of life, is not of the Father but is of the world. And the world passes away, and the lust of it; but he who does the will of God abides for ever" (1 John 2:15-17).*

The flesh opposes the Holy Spirit. The Bible says,

"But I say, walk by the Spirit, and do not gratify the desires of the flesh. For the desires of the flesh are against the Spirit, and the desires of the Spirit are against the flesh; for these are opposed to each other, to prevent you from doing what you would. But if you are led by the Spirit you are not under the law. Now the works of the flesh are plain: fornication, impurity, licentiousness, idolatry, sorcery, enmity, strife, jealousy, anger, selfishness, dissension, party spirit, envy, drunkenness, carousing, and the like. I warn you, as I warned you before, that those who do such things shall not inherit the kingdom of God. But the fruit of the Spirit is love, joy, peace, patience, kindness, goodness, faithfulness, gentleness, self-control; against such there is no law. And those who belong to Christ Jesus have crucified the flesh with its passions and desires" (Galatians 5:16-24).

The devil opposes the Son, the Lord Jesus. The Bible says,

"Then Jesus was led up by the Spirit into the wilderness to be tempted by the devil. And he fasted forty days and forty nights, and afterward he was hungry. And the tempter came and said to him, 'If you are the Son of God, command these stones to become loaves of bread.' But he answered, 'It is written, "Man shall not live by bread alone, but by every word that proceeds from the mouth of God."' Then the devil took him to the holy city, and set him on the pinnacle of the temple, and said to him, 'If you are the Son of God, throw yourself down; for it is written, "He will give his angels charge of you," and "on their hands they will bear you up, lest you strike your foot against a stone."' Jesus said to him, 'Again it is written, "You shall not tempt the Lord your God."' Again, the devil took him to a very high mountain, and showed him all the kingdoms of the world and the glory of them; and he said to him, 'All these I will give you, if you will fall down and worship me.' Then Jesus said to him, 'Be gone, Satan! For it is written, "You shall worship the Lord your God and him only shall you serve."' Then the devil left him, and behold, angels came and ministered to him" (Matthew 4:1-11).

By his death on the cross Jesus won a far-reaching and final victory over the totality of the satanic trinity. The world was judged on the cross. The apostle Paul said,

> "But far be it from me to glory except in the cross of our Lord Jesus Christ, by which the world has been crucified to me, and I to the world" (Galatians 6:14).

The flesh was judged on the cross. The Bible says,

> "We know that our old self was crucified with him so that the sinful body might be destroyed, and we might no longer be enslaved to sin" (Romans 6:6).

> "I have been crucified with Christ; it is no longer I who live, but Christ who lives in me; and the life I now live in the flesh I live by faith in the Son of God, who loved me and gave himself for me" (Galatians 2:20).

The devil and his hosts were defeated on the cross. The Bible says,

> "He disarmed principalities and powers and made a public example of them, triumphing over them in him (that is, the cross)" (Colossians 2:15).

> "The ruler of this world is judged" (John 16:11).

The death of Christ is God's perfect answer to the problem of the devil's trinity.

GOD'S VIEW OF THE WORK OF THE CROSS

Jesus died in the sinner's place on the cross. That is great. That is wonderful. He disarmed principalities and powers and made a public show of them. The devil and his whole kingdom felt the impact of that victory. The cross was a contest for eternal supremacy. Two mighty princes went there to the cross - Prince Jesus and Prince

Satan. By rendering perfect obedience to the Lord God, Jesus gave the father of disobedience a technical knock-out and secured victory once and for all. The Bible says,

> *"Since therefore the children share in flesh and blood, he himself likewise partook of the same nature, that through death he might destroy him who has the power of death, that is, the devil"* (Hebrews 2:14).

How did the Father react to this? He reacted with the fullest approval. He did this by raising Jesus up from the dead. The resurrection of Jesus Christ from the dead is God's stamp of approval on the work of Jesus on the cross. The Bible says,

> *"God raised him up"* (Acts 2:24).

> *"God raised the Lord"* (1 Corinthians 6:14).

There is an empty tomb to testify to the resurrection of the Lord Jesus, and this empty tomb says, "God was satisfied with the work of redemption accomplished by His Son on the cross."

What of the other religious leaders? Well, He did not raise them up. He abandoned them in the grave until this day to show that what they started was something totally of their own creation and in rebellion to Him. He has allowed them to remain in the grave until that day when the dead, great and small, shall stand before the Lord Jesus for judgment. Indeed, all these religious leaders shall be raised on the last day to face Jesus the Chief Judge on that Day!

THE INDISPENSABLE RESURRECTION

Had Jesus not risen from the dead, He would have passed for a great religious leader like Buddha, Mohammed, and the others. He would have been conquered by death and held in bondage until now. However, Jesus rose from the dead. His resurrection placed Him in a special position. There is none like Him. There never will be any other like Him. There need be no other one like Him. His resurrection was no fancy. He was seen by many after His resurrection. The Word of the Lord says,

> "*He was raised on the third day in accordance with the Scriptures, and that he appeared to Cephas, then to the Twelve. Then he appeared to more than five hundred brethren at one time, most of whom are still alive, though some have fallen asleep. Then he appeared to James, then to all the apostles*" (I Corinthians 15:4-7).

Then He appeared to Saul the great persecutor of Christians and changed him into Paul, the great apostle. Then in 1966, He appeared to me. He came into my room, into the darkness of my life, picked me up, changed me, and I have never been the same. Even more recently, this very afternoon, as I was driving, He got into the car, talked with me, and I talked with Him. He is indeed alive!

JESUS - GOD'S ONLY WAY OF SALVATION

Jesus is the only Way back to God. He said,

> "*I am the way, and the truth, and the life; NO ONE COMES TO THE FATHER, BUT BY ME*" (*John 14:6*).

The Word of God says about Christ,

> "*And there is salvation in no one else, for there is NO OTHER NAME under heaven given among men by which we must be saved*" (*Acts 4:12*).

> "*For there is one God, and there is ONE MEDIATOR between God and men, the man Christ Jesus, who gave himself as a ransom for all*" (*1 Timothy 2:5-6*).

Was Jesus mistaken when He said that He was the only Way? Are the Scriptures mistaken when they testify to the fact that He is the only Way? If Jesus was mistaken and the Scriptures are false, then Christianity must be the greatest deception, and Jesus the greatest liar that ever lived. He would, however, have to be a liar who lived a perfectly righteous life, and whose lies raised Him from the dead. He would be a liar whose life and death changed the lives of multitudes, including mine!

But Jesus was not a liar. The testimony of the Scriptures is true. He indeed is God's one Way of life. Anyone who thinks that he can find salvation outside of the Lord Jesus, is either deceiving himself or he has allowed himself to be deceived.

My dear reader, do not allow yourself to be deceived. Do not deceive yourself. If you must see God some day, if you must spend eternity in the security of heaven, then you had better know and act upon the fact that Jesus is God's one and only Way of salvation. Listen again to the words of Jesus,

> *"No one has ascended into heaven but he who descended from heaven, the Son of man. And as Moses lifted up the serpent in the wilderness, so must the Son of man be lifted up, that whoever believes in him may have eternal life"* (John 3:13-15).

You should become part of that "whoever". God has included you there. Do not exclude yourself.

THE WAY OUT OF THE OLD CREATION

As we have seen, the old creation became, through sin, something abominable that God could not patch up or mend. He decided to get rid of it entirely. God summed up all that was of the old creation in Christ and brought it to an end, once and for all in Christ, on the cross. Adam was the head of the race. He sinned and, therefore, brought a false life to all his descendants. All his descendants, having been born into the old life, have only one way out of it, through death. The only way out of the old life is through death.

However, in order that there might be hope, it could not be just any death. It had to be a special death. That is why when Jesus died, He took with Him the old creation to the cross, and when He died, He brought the old creation legally to death. He became the last Adam to bring to an end all that the first Adam, out of rebellion, had brought into existence.

We repeat that all died in Christ. The death of Christ was an all-inclusive death.

AN ALL-INCLUSIVE RESURRECTION

The purpose of God in redemption was that all that was lost in Adam might be regained in Christ. He had it in mind that all of the inanimate and all of the animate world might come "to life" in Christ.

For that part of creation that has not been given free will, the death of Christ purchased a redemption that is already visible and that will be fully visible when Christ returns. There may still be groans now: earthquakes, floods, hostility amongst animals. ... As the Bible says,

> "For the creation was subjected to futility, not of its own will but by
> the will of him who subjected it in hope; because the creation itself
> will be set free from its bondage to decay and obtain the glorious
> liberty of the children of God" (Romans 8:20-21).

A day is coming when the groaning and decay will end. When the Lord Jesus comes in all His glory, the liberation of creation, which has now been purchased, will be fully evident there will be no earthquakes, storms, floods, and other natural calamities. There will be perfect peace and harmony in the animal world,

> "The wolf and the lamb shall feed together, the lion shall eat straw like
> the ox; and dust shall be the serpent's food. They shall not hurt or
> destroy in all my holy mountain" (Isaiah 65:25).

God will create new heavens and a new earth, and the former things shall be remembered no more (Isaiah 65:17). All these shall be possible because all of the old creation was summed up in the death and the resurrection of Christ.

What of man, the apex of creation? Is he automatically included in the resurrection of Christ? The answer is: "No!" God has included all men in the death of His Son on the cross, but it is only those who reject sin and receive Him who are included in the resurrection. Resurrection life is a life of obedience. How can God include people in that life who have not given up rebellion? Rejecting Christ either actively or passively is rebellion. Rebellion brought the first creation into utter ruin. He is ensuring that all who enter into the new creation have given up all desire to rebel, even in the slightest way.

Dear reader, if you want to be part of the new creation, you must accept God's way out of the old creation and enter the new creation on God's own condition. Will you do that today?

FINALLY

Some people specialize in blaming Adam for the fall, the ruin of the old creation. No one will go to hell because Adam sinned. No one will perish because he was born with a sin-nature. God has settled that problem in a master way by the death and resurrection of His Son.

People will, however, perish for not receiving God's way out of the old creation. The Lord Jesus said about the Holy Spirit,

> *"And when he comes, he will convice the world concerning sin and righteousness and judgment: concerning sin, because they do not believe in me" (John 16:8).*

> *"And this is the judgment, that the light has come into the world, and men loved darkness rather than light, because their deeds were evil" (John 3:19).*

Two ways are open before you: the way of life in Christ or the way of death outside of Him. We offer to you today the choice between the Lord Jesus and the devil, between eternal life and eternal death, between heaven and hell, between God's love and God's wrath. The offer is from God. The choice is yours. You must make your choice yourself, and after you have made your choice, you must bear the consequences of that choice throughout all time and all eternity. You do well to act wisely.

WITHOUT CHRIST:

- Without Christ, man would be a corpse waiting to be thrown into the lake of fire.
- Without Christ, the old sacrificial system would continue without effect.
- Without Christ, God's love for the world would be unknown and not experienced.
- Without Christ, there would be no new covenant between God and man by which God forgives sinners and remembers their sins no more.
- Without Christ, the film of the human life with its tragic scenes would remain, waiting to be projected on the Judgment Day.
- Without Christ, there would be no salvation from the consequences of sin.
- Without Christ, there would be no deliverance from the power of sin day by day.
- Without Christ, man would live in the presence of sin eternally.
- Without Christ, man would live perpetually and hopelessly under the law.
- Without Christ, the devil, the world and the flesh would reign unchallenged.
- Without Christ, man would be without a Saviour and without hope.
- Without Christ, the whole creation would remain in tragic bondage.
- Thanks be to God the Father for Jesus and His victorious work.

Amen.

QUESTIONS

Answer the questions with clear Bible passages to support your answers.

1. What did God do to clothe Adam and Eve after they had sinned?
2. Adam and Eve provided leaves for their clothing, while God shed blood. What do you see here about justification by works and justification by faith in the blood that was shed?
3. When the angel passed through the land of Egypt, he passed through Egyptian houses killing the first-born and passed over the houses of the children of Israel, sparing them. What made the difference between the Egyptians and the Israelites?
4. Why is the shedding of blood indispensable for the forgiveness of sin?
5. What were the qualifications that the Passover Lamb had to meet?
6. How did Jesus satisfy the requirements of God's Passover Lamb?
7. Why was Jesus born?
8. Was Jesus forced to die?
9. Why did Jesus die?
10. What is salvation: (a) in the past? (b) in the present? (c) in the future?
11. How did the death of Christ affect the law?
12. What was deficient in the sacrificial system of the Old Testament?
13. Why is it an abomination before God to offer blood sacrifices today?
14. Who are the members of the satanic trinity?
15. Whom does each member of the satanic trinity oppose?
16. Show clearly how the death of Christ affected the satanic trinity.
17. Was God satisfied with the work of Christ on the cross? If yes, how did He manifest His approval?

18. What evidence do you have: (a) from the lives of others ... (b) from your own life, that the resurrection is an absolute reality?

19. How many ways are there for lost sinners to go back to God the Father? Explain your answer.

20. What hope is there for sincere people who are seeking salvation outside of Jesus?

21. What is the one way that is open to all people to get them out of the old creation? Has anyone any choice about that way?

22. Who is included in the resurrection of Jesus?

23. What hope is there for the rest of the old creation outside of Christ?

4

THE NEW CREATION

We have already seen that Jesus did not only die. He rose again from the dead. When Jesus went to the cross, He took all of the old creation that is willing to be identified with Him in His death. When He rose from the dead, He brought from death to life all of the old creation that is willing to be identified with Him in His resurrection. The new creation is possible because of the resurrection of Christ.

We said earlier on that the dead man died. He was dead in Adam. He died again in Christ. The dead man that died in Christ can also come to life in Christ; for Jesus is not only the last Adam. He is also the second Adam - the starting point of a humanity called the sons of God. The Bible says,

> *"Therefore, if any one is in Christ, he is a new creation, the old has passed away, behold, the new has come"* (II Corinthians 5:17).

The new life is radically different from the old life, so much so that there can be no comparison whatsoever. The new life in Christ is not personal reformation of character. It is no suppression of sinful desires. It is not a human attempt to live by some principles like keeping the demands of one law code or the other.

The new life is God's supernatural life imparted to any human being whose old life has been brought to an end by union with Christ in His death on the cross. The new life is Jesus' resurrection life imparted by the Holy Spirit to those who become one with Him in His triumphant resurrection.

The new life that is received in Christ is something exceedingly greater than what Adam lost when he sinned. The new life in Christ has all that Adam, through consistent obedience to the Lord, was to become. The one who is recreated in Christ Jesus is far better placed in relationship with God than Adam was before the fall. The new man in Christ possesses potentials that Adam had, and more.

HOW TO BECOME A NEW CREATION.

THE ABILITY OF GOD TO IMPART NEW LIFE

The Bible says,

> *"To all who received him, who believed in his name, he gave power to become children of God; who were born, not of blood nor of the will of the flesh nor of the will of man, but of God" (John 1:12-13).*

The Lord Jesus said,

> *"Truly, truly, I say to you, unless one is born anew, he cannot see the kingdom of God" (John 3:3).*

> *"Truly, truly, I say to you, unless one is born of water and the Spirit, he cannot enter the kingdom of God" (John 3:5).*

> *"For God so loved the world that he gave his only Son, that whoever believes in him should not perish but have eternal life" (John 3:16).*

> *"Come to me, all who labour and are heavy laden, and I will give you rest" (Matthew 11:28).*

"He who believes and is baptized will be saved" (Mark 16:16).

"Repent, and be baptized every one of you in the name of Jesus Christ for the forgiveness of your sins; and you shall receive the gift of the Holy Spirit" (Acts 2:38).

"If you confess with your lips that Jesus is Lord and believe in your heart that God raised him from the dead, you will be saved. For man believes with his heart and so is justified, and he confesses with his lips and so is saved" (Romans 10:9-10).

"For, every one who calls upon the name of the Lord will be saved" (Romans 10:13).

GOD'S ABILITY TO ACT AT ONCE

The moment when any individual repents towards God and puts his faith in the Lord Jesus, God instantaneously and immediately gives him power to become a child of God. A sinner is justified at the split second when he calls upon the Lord Jesus to save him. It may take preparation, battling, weighing the pros and the cons by the sinner under conviction, but from the very moment that with faith in the Lord Jesus, he asks for pardon and salvation, he receives both from the Lord, and more. God does not need time to prepare. God is always ready. God in Christ Jesus never comes into anyone's heart slowly. He never takes minutes or days to make one a new creation. The hymn writer wrote, "And so quickly the transaction was made when as a sinner I believed." My dear friend, I want to let you know that within a matter of seconds you can pass from death unto life in Jesus Christ. You can cease to be the son of the devil and become God's child within seconds.

THE INDISPENSABLE WHOLE-HEARTEDNESS

Although man needs no public announcement of his commitment to the Lord Jesus in order to be justified, Jesus will not accept those who want to deal with Him only in private. He said,

> "*And I tell you, every one who acknowledges me before men, the Son of man also will acknowledge before the angels of God; but he who denies me before men will be denied before the angels of God*"
> (Luke 12:8-9).

Jesus will never accept anyone today whom He will not accept until the end. He is not moved by human words. He weighs human hearts. At the very beginning of His ministry the Word of God says of Him,

> "*Now when he was in Jerusalem at the Passover feast, many believed in his name when they saw the signs which he did; but Jesus did not trust himself to them, because he knew all men and needed no one to bear witness of man; for he himself knew what was in man*"
> (John 2:23-25).

Yes, the Lord knows what is in man, not only for now, but for all time. The whole attitude of the human heart; past, present and future is bare before Him. He will have nothing to do with people in whose hearts He sees no whole-heartedness, both now and in the future. He will not be tricked.

Although man does not need to be baptized in order to be justified, Jesus will not receive anyone who says to Him, "Lord, I will come to You so that I may be forgiven, but I will not obey Your command to be baptized. That command is not for me." Jesus said, "He who believes and is baptized shall be saved." He means it. Believe, then be baptized, and then you will be saved.

Although no one needs to carry out restitution in order to be forgiven, the Lord cannot receive anyone who is prepared to sit on stolen things and make noise, saying that he is saved. The new life demands that the old life be brought radically to an end.

The Lord Jesus won in the mighty conflict with the devil by obeying God. He will not enter the hearts of people who are not prepared to be obedient. Anyone who has reservations about the Lord Jesus and His Word, either in part or in whole, can make some decisions for Christ, weep,... but will remain unjustified. God looks at the heart.

He accepts only those who will come to Him in a total way. To come to Jesus on man's own conditions is rebellion.

There are many who pass for born again believers, for saved people, for true Christians ... who are not. They have never touched God. The Bible says that as many as touched Him were made whole. No one can touch Jesus conditionally and become a partaker of the divine nature. The rich young ruler was sent away. He was good. He was willing and he was humble, but he was half-hearted, and Jesus could not help him.

Jesus asked people to count the cost. Dear friend, have you counted the cost? The Lord said,

> "Unless you repent you will all likewise perish" (Luke 13:3).

> "And some one said to him, 'Lord, will those who are saved be few?' And he said to them, 'Strive to enter by the narrow door; for many, I tell you, will seek to enter and will not be able'" (Luke 13:23-24).

Justification is by faith, and by faith alone, but genuine faith embraces the Lord Jesus and His Word, and has no reservations whatsoever. My dear reader, do you have any reservations in your heart about the Lord Jesus or some of His commands? If there are such reservations, be careful. Such reservations indicate the fact that your heart is divided, and Jesus has no use for divided hearts. Are you clinging to something that separates you from the life of the Lord Jesus? Is that thing worth all the glory of heaven that you are about to throw away? Will that thing satisfy your heart when in the end you are in hell? Think again, for "What will it profit a man if he should gain the whole world and lose his soul?" What can a man give in exchange for his soul? What can you give in exchange for your soul?

REPENTANCE

Repentance is a change of mind. The normal sinner's mind is blinded by the devil. The Bible says,

> *"And even if our gospel is veiled, it is veiled only to those who are
> perishing. In their case the god of this world has blinded the minds
> of the unbelievers, to keep them from seeing the light of the gospel
> of the glory of Christ, who is the likeness of God" (II Corinthians
> 4:3-4).*

The devil holds men's minds in captivity. However, the devil's power
over men's minds is powerless against the Lord Jesus, who is the light
of the world. The Bible says,

> *"The light shines in the darkness, and the darkness has not overcome it"*
> *(John 1:5).*

In spite of all of Satan's work in blinding men's hearts, the Holy Spirit
is able to penetrate the darkened mind and call men to repentance.
Man, on his own, unaided by the Holy Spirit, cannot repent. The
Bible says,

> *"Then to the Gentiles also God has granted repentance unto life"* (Acts
> 11: 18).

> *"God may perhaps grant that they will repent and come to know the
> truth, and they may escape from the snare of the devil, after being
> captured by him to do his will"* (II Timothy 2:25-26).

If God did not grant repentance, the unbeliever would hear the
Word, understand the grammar and the facts of it, but not understand the spiritual truth there-embodied, and so remain in captivity.
But when God grants repentance, there is a change of mind, a change
of mind towards God, a change of mind towards the devil, a change
of mind towards the world, a change of mind towards the church....
Before, God was seen as an interferer, but the changed mind loves
God and wants Him. Before, the devil was accepted actively or
passively; now, he is dreaded. Before, sin was considered good or only
a mistake, but now, it is known to be all-terrible. Before, the world
and its passing glories were treasures; now, it is known for what it is
vain and passing. Before, the body of Christ, the believers were

regarded with contempt; now, they are seen as utterly precious. Repentance leads to a knowledge of the truth, and truth leads people to come to their senses. In their proper senses they escape the snare of the devil, whose captives they have been, and whose will they have done until now. They are now prepared to turn to Christ.

FAITH IN THE LORD JESUS

When a person repents towards God, he is not yet a believer. He must now have faith in the Lord Jesus. The apostle Paul told the Ephesian elders,

> *"I did not shrink from declaring to you anything that was profitable, and teaching you in public and from house to house, testifying both to Jews and to Greeks of REPENTANCE TO GOD AND FAITH IN OUR LORD JESUS CHRIST"* (Acts 20:20-21).

If the repentance is not genuine, there will be no real faith in the Lord Jesus. False repentance will lead to a false faith, and to a false conversion experience.

When a person repents towards God, he is not yet a believer. He must have faith in Christ; he must receive the Lord Jesus. The Bible says,

> *"But to all who received him, who believed in his name, he gave power to become children of God"* (John 1:12).

And the Lord said,

> *"Behold, I stand at the door and knock; if any one hears my voice and opens the door, I will come in to him and eat with him, and he with me"* (Revelation 3:20).

When a person repents towards God and receives the Lord Jesus, he is born again from above by the power of the Holy Spirit. His heart and mind are illuminated by the light of God's presence, and he becomes a partaker of divine nature.

RECEIVING THE LORD JESUS

You can receive the Lord Jesus right now by praying in the following lines - or in other words of your choosing. "Lord God, I have personally sinned against You in my thoughts, in my words and in my actions. Nothing that I do on my own can take away my sin. I deserve to go to hell. But You loved a wretched sinner like me and sent Your Son Jesus Christ to die in my place on the cross. I recognize that only Jesus can save me. I now surrender my life to Him completely, without reserve. Take away all my sins and send the Lord Jesus to come into my heart right now as my personal Saviour and Lord. I give You my life to do with it as You like. I will follow You at any cost. Thank You for hearing my prayer and saving me."

If you prayed the above prayer sincerely, then Jesus has come into your heart and you have immediately become a child of God. Glory be to the Lord!

THE MARKS OF THE CONVERTED

The fundamental mark of the converted is that they love Jesus and love Him without any reservation. The converted also love the others who belong to the Lord. So the basic mark is a vertical love for God and a horizontal love for the brethren. This mark distinguishes all true believers from the rest of the world.

Another basic mark of conversion is a commitment to follow the Lord Jesus come what may. This means that the one in whom Jesus dwells is prepared to hear His voice and act accordingly in obedience. The Lord Jesus said to the Pharisees,

> "You do not believe, because you do not belong to my sheep. My sheep hear my voice, and I know them, and they follow me" (John 10:26-27).

THE STANDING OF THE NEW CREATION

JUSTIFICATION

Justification is the rendering of a guilty person not guilty before a judge. Our sin had made us guilty before God, but through His death on the cross, Christ made it possible for us to stand before God "just as if we never sinned."

> *"We are now justified by his blood"* (Romans 5:9).

Justification makes it possible for sinners to have peace with God, for,

> *"Since we are justified by faith, we have peace with God"* (Romans 5:1).

A young man committed a very grievous offence against the law of his country. He was brought before the judge, tried and found guilty. His punishment was stated: death by hanging! As he was about to move to the place of his death, the judge's only son stepped forward and offered to be punished in the place of the man who had committed the crime. He was stripped and hanged on the tree instead of the young man. The judge's son bore the penalty, but the young man was justified. He was asked to go away just as if he never committed the offence. He was justified because another took his place. Christ did a similar thing. We, too, like the young man, have sinned very grievously. By rebellion we have committed high treason against the government of heaven. We have been tried by God, the righteous Judge and found guilty, and our punishment (eternal hell) declared.

However, Jesus, out of love for us, took our place and was hanged on the cross where we ought to have been hanged. In this way, God's demand that sin must be punished was met and He now sees us as a free people who have never sinned. This is God's method of setting people free from the penalty of sin. It is such a costly way that His

Son was sacrificed for us. Yes, Jesus paid the price for us. The Word of God says,

> *"The Lord has laid on him the iniquity of us all"* (Isaiah 53:6).

> *"For Christ also died for sins once for all, the righteous for the unrighteous, that he might bring us to God"* (1 Peter 3:18),

and

> *"For our sake he made him to be sin who knew no sin, so that in him we might become the righteousness of God"* (II Corinthians 5:21).

REDEMPTION

Redemption is the setting free of a person who is held in bondage through the payment of a ransom. Sin makes the sinner a prisoner, and sin has a penalty. By His death on the cross, Jesus set the sinner free from both the penalty and the power of sin by paying a price.

> *"Christ redeemed us from the curse of the law, having become a curse for us" (Galatians 3:13).*

> *"Jesus Christ, who gave himself for us to redeem us from all iniquity" (Titus 2:14).*

> *"They are justified by his grace as a gift, through the redemption which is in Christ Jesus" (Romans 3:24).*

> *"In him we have redemption through his blood, the forgiveness of our trespasses, according to the riches of his grace" (Ephesians 1:7).*

Imagine a slave market. There are slave owners with chained slaves. These slaves are to be sold to some far off country. Because they are chained, they cannot set themselves free. Suddenly, a big boss comes into the slave market, pays the price of each slave, takes away the chains, and declares the slaves free. How wonderful!

Jesus did that! We were Satan's slaves and imprisoned by him, and we were meant to share his eternal home (hell) with him. On the cross, Jesus paid the price for our liberation. He now declares all of us who turn from sin to Him free. On the cross, Jesus paid the price for our liberation and declares us free. The free slave requires a new home. Jesus also made provision for this by His death on the cross. We are lifted out of the kingdom of our former master (Satan), and transferred into an entirely new Kingdom which is His. The Bible says,

"He has delivered us from the dominion of darkness and transferred us to the kingdom of his beloved Son, in whom we have redemption, the forgiveness of sins" (Colossians 1:13-14).

The story is told of a young man who fell into a pit. Many people passed by, and, in order to be safe, stood at a comfortable distance from the pit. From that distance, they began to try and sympathize with him. Some made suggestions to him about how he could get out of the pit. One person said to him, "Believe that there is one God and you will be out of the pit." The man in the pit replied that he had never doubted the fact that there is one true God. He further added that he believed absolutely in the existence of God. That, however, did not get him out of the pit. Another person told him that all that was required to get him out of the pit was frequent fasts and many prayers each day. He tried to pray, and since there was no food in the pit, fasting posed no problem to him. This also failed to get him out of the pit. The third person suggested that all he needed was to attend church services in a particular denominational church building and pay all his contributions and all would be well. He replied that he did in fact belong to that denomination, and that he was a financial member in the said church. However, since he was in the pit, he needed to get out of it in order to be able to attend church services and bring his financial position in the church up to date. The man advising asked, "Are you sure that you are baptized and confirmed? That is all important for getting you out of the pit." He replied that he was duly baptized and confirmed and that his Christian name was John, and that, before falling into the pit, he partook regularly of the Holy Communion. He then added with deep frustration, "But all this does not seem to be able to get me out of this pit."

Finally, someone great and noble came along. He went very close to the pit and saw the fallen man's plight. He took rags and wore them and then entered the pit. Inside the pit he lifted up the fallen man out of the pit. In the process of lifting him out, he bruised himself and blood flowed out. Outside the pit, he looked at the man who had fallen inside the pit. He was out of the pit, but clothed in rags. He had compassion on him, took the dirty clothes off his body, and put on him his own rich clothing, saying to the man, "I can get others for myself."

Jesus did just that. All human beings had fallen into "the pit of sin." All human, philosophical and religious attempts at getting man out of that pit had failed. As man was totally helpless, God looked down from heaven, had compassion on man, put aside His glory as God, took upon Himself our humanity, came right into the human mess and, by His death on the cross, paid for our redemption, and now clothes redeemed people with His glory.

RECONCILIATION

Reconciliation is the making of peace between enemies. Because of sin, man became an enemy of God. As an enemy of God, man needed to be reconciled to God. Christ's death on the cross healed that enmity. God, however, never changed His attitude towards man. It is man who, through rebellion, changed his attitude towards God. Repentance is the change of this wrong attitude, and reconciliation brings the man whose attitude has been changed through repentance into vital fellowship with God. The death of Christ on the cross provided the way by which rebellious man can get back into fellowship with God.

The Bible says,

> *"While we were still weak, at the right time Christ died for the*

ungodly. Why, one will hardly die for a righteous man though perhaps for a good man one will dare even to die. But God shows his love for us in that while we were yet sinners Christ died for us" (Romans 5:6-8).

"While we were enemies we were reconciled to God by the death of his Son" (Romans 5:10).

"God, who through Christ reconciled us to himself" (II Corinthians 5:18).

Because we have been reconciled to God, the Bible says,

"But now in Christ Jesus you who once were far off have been brought near in the blood of Christ" (Ephesians 2:13).

"For through him we both have access in one Spirit to the Father" (Ephesians 2:18).

So because of the death of Christ, the broken relationship between man and God has been restored. The veil that separated the Holy Place from the Holy of Holies in the Temple was torn, to show the fact that man can come to God by Jesus and be accepted. This is very good news.

The reconciliation that was accomplished by the death of Christ was not only a reconciliation of man with God. It was also a reconciliation of man with man. In the Lord Jesus, colour, national, tribal, class ... barriers are broken down. The Bible says,

"For in Christ Jesus you are all sons of God, through faith. For as many of you as were baptized into Christ have put on Christ. There is neither Jew nor Greek, there is neither slave nor free, there is neither male nor female; for you are all one in Christ Jesus" (Galatians 3:26-28).

"Do not lie to one another, seeing that you have put off the old nature

> *with its practices and have put on the new nature, which is being*
> *renewed in knowledge after the image of its creator. Here there*
> *cannot be Greek and Jew, circumcised and uncircumcised,*
> *barbarian, Scythian, slave, free man, but Christ is all, and in all"*
> *(Colossians 3:9-11).*

Yes, indeed in Christ, barriers are broken. This is reality and not theory. Let me illustrate it with a true story. I was visiting one country on a scientific tour. At the earliest opportunity, I made contact with the believers and was invited to speak at a meeting arranged particularly for the wives of University teachers. The Lord moved at the meeting and many were blessed. At the close of the meeting, an elegant lady of about forty-five asked if she could have a private talk with me. We arranged a meeting for the next day. At that meeting, I just sat down for two hours while she poured out her sad story. She had been married for twenty five years. She was a virgin at the time of their marriage, and all through her life her husband was the only man in her life. She had loved him and trusted him. However, five years before then she discovered that he had been untrue to her for all their years together, and had children in secret with other women. "I have seen the children and they all resemble him," she said. From then on her heart had been broken and her deep love for him had turned into bitter hatred. He had apologized and was truly repentant, but her heart had remained closed to him. Then she added, "Everyday I sit at table opposite him, and the sight of him makes me feel like ending my life, and his." As she spoke, at some point, this sophisticated and well educated lady became the very embodiment of anger, and she stood up and paced the room, talking aloud about the man's unfaithfulness. I did not know what I could do. So I prayed and asked the Lord Jesus to be specially close to me and show me what to do. I also asked the Lord God to calm down the woman so that I could talk to her. After some time, she sat down and said, "We have money, position, respect, everything, but, finally, I have nothing." I then talked to her, not about the husband, but about herself. I made her see that she was a sinner by nature, and that her bitterness over the years was a clear evidence of her sin. I further showed her that both she and her husband were sinners and lost. Her husband's sinful nature manifested itself in adultery, and hers in bitterness. There was really no difference between them before the Lord. The Holy Spirit used those words to convict her, and soon she was weeping before God over her sin. I enabled her to see Jesus as the sin Bearer and helped her to receive Him. It was wonderful. Her tears turned to laughter, and, as she stood up to go, she said to me, "I am going home to tell my husband that because of the death of Christ for us, I love him and forgive him unconditionally." She left the room a transformed woman, and I fell on my knees to thank the Lord God who in Christ reconciles people to Himself and to each other. Glory be to God for His wonderful reconciliation!

HE IS BORN AGAIN

The new creature is described as born again. In his first birth, he was born into the old creation. He died in Christ and, thereby, passed out of the old creation. By resurrection with Christ he receives God's supernatural life. He is born again from above (from heaven, from God). It is totally a supernatural transaction carried out by God in the life of the willing person. The Bible says,

> "Truly, truly, I say to you, unless one is born anew (from above), he
> cannot see the kingdom of God" (John 3:3).

In his first birth, he came as a fallen creature into the family of Satan. He died with Christ out of that family, in order to be born again into the family of God. The Bible says,

> "Blessed be the God and Father of our Lord Jesus Christ! By his great
> mercy we have been born anew to a living hope through the
> resurrection of Jesus Christ from the dead" (1 Peter 1:3).

All who have received the Lord Jesus are born again people. It is not something that they can do by themselves. It is God's supernatural work carried out in people at the moment when they receive the Lord Jesus as their Lord and Saviour. It is nothing that can be done by the will of man. It must be done by God. The Bible says,

> *"But to all who received him, who believed in his name, he gave*
> *power to become children of God; who were born, not of blood nor*
> *of the will of the flesh nor of the will of man, but of God"* (John
> 1:12-13).

This new birth must be experienced at the personal level. No amount of theoretical knowledge will help a man. He must be born again. The need for this personal experience of the Lord Jesus as personal Saviour is seen in the following testimony borne by a lady we know. She says, "I was born into a religious family, my father being a church minister. In infancy, I was duly "baptized" and when I came of age, I was confirmed. I dutifully attended Sunday School classes and had nothing against God or against Jesus Christ. In fact, I loved God in a vague kind of way, although I did not know Him! While I was in the Secondary School, I was an active member of our denominational students' movement, and maintained a high moral standard. After the Secondary School, I got myself well-grounded in church-going, and even joined the choir and the Christian Youth group, where I was elected a committee member. In the group, we carried out, among other things, hospital and prison visitation. We were supposed to evangelize people (even though we ourselves needed to be evangelized). Church-going had become such an integral part of my being that I felt ill whenever I could not go to church for one reason or the other. Even after dancing until the early hours of Sunday morning, I always managed to go to church, even though that meant that at times I slept during most of the service. With such involvement and zeal in religious things, and not knowing that there was something more in the Christian life, I thought myself a very good Christian. Some of my friends even thought that I was getting too involved with religion.

This state of things continued until I went abroad to study. There, I joined the Christian group as usual. I was, however, surprised that the members of this group talked and lived as if Jesus was real to them and meant everything in the whole world to them. They even claimed to talk to Him personally. I would have rejected their claims as presumptuous, had it not been for the fact that their lives showed that they possessed something positive, which I lacked, and which they attributed to the inner working of Jesus in their lives. As I continued in that union, I was shown my need of a personal relationship with Jesus Christ. I then repented of my sin and sins and turned my whole heart and life over to the Lord Jesus, and begged Him to come and live in me. He did come into my heart and life, and my life and Christian involvement then took on a new dimension. I have been born again from above since that day on which I received the Lord Jesus, and it is my joy to serve Him."

HE IS SAVED

Although man was lost and needed to be saved, and although the Father wanted him saved, this did not put any obligation on the Lord Jesus. All that He did for the salvation of sinners was motivated by love. As the Father so loved the world that He gave His Son for its salvation, so also did the Lord Jesus so love the world that He gave Himself away for its salvation.

In all His teaching, miracles and life, Jesus was love incarnate. He loved the most unlovable, touched the most untouchable and made friends with the rejects of the society. Think of the Samaritan woman at the well who had been rejected by five husbands and was trying it out with a sixth man when she met Jesus. Each of these men saw her as something to be used and then be rejected, but Jesus loved her with an all-encompassing love that forgave her and gave her a fresh start and a bright future. Think of the woman caught in adultery. Her neighbours judged her and wanted her dead, but Jesus looked at her, loved her and saved her from death by stoning and from eternal fire. So mighty was His love for her that it transformed her life. Think of the tax collector, Zacchaeus, who was totally despised by all for his wicked ways; yet Jesus loved him and paid him a personal visit that led to his conversion and salvation. There is no sinner that Jesus does not love and does not want to save. Let me illustrate this by a personal experience.

On the 24th of December 1970, while I was a post-graduate student at Makerere University, Kampala, I wondered how best I could spend the Christmas Eve. I later decided to spend the day in prayer and asked the Lord to send people who needed to hear about the salvation of God. At seven o'clock that evening, I set out on one of the streets of Kampala, telling everyone whom I could persuade to listen to me about the love of Christ revealed by His death on the cross. At eleven p.m. as I was returning to the University campus, I stopped by to tell Brother Laban Jumba, who had promised to pray for me, how the evangelism had gone on. After a brief talk with him, I began to hurry home as it was rather late. A night-watchman stopped me and asked about my identity. I told him whom I was and what I had been doing. I further inquired of him if he would let me tell him something about the mighty rescue operation of God. Upon obtaining his permission, I briefly told him about man's need and the love of God as revealed in the incarnation, death and resurrection of Jesus Christ. I further pressed upon him his own need of being saved from the coming wrath of God. Upon hearing this, my friend, whom I prefer to call Mr. X, asked me, "Can God receive a wretched sinner like me? Can He save one as sinful as I am?" He then went on to tell me the sad story of his life. This is what he said: "I was a police officer, but when I found that soldiers earned more money and had more privileges than policemen, I resigned from the police force and joined the army. After some time I thought that the best way to make money quickly was by becoming a businessman. I, therefore, resigned from the army and set up a business. When I began to make money, many women came into my life, and each woman took away more money from me than the previous one. Finally, I became broke and my business collapsed. As a penniless man I decided to seek employment as a night-watchman."

Then he looked at me with tears in his eyes and asked again, *"Can Jesus receive a wretched sinner like me?"* At that moment I saw in a new way the glory of the all-loving Christ, whose love is so great that He accepts and receives all kinds of repentant sinners, irrespective of the degree of their sin. I gladly told him that Jesus was just too willing to receive him there and then, if he would repent and turn to Him. So we bowed in prayer and Mr. X confessed his sins to God, asked for forgiveness and, then, asked Jesus to come into his life as his Saviour and Lord. He was saved immediately he received the Lord Jesus.

The Bible says,

> "*For by grace you have been saved through faith; and this is not your own doing, it is the gift of God*" (Ephesians 2:8).

He was saved from the consequences of sin immediately he believed. That salvation is a finished fact and so he stands in it. Because of its reality and certainty, it enables the saved person to trust the Lord Jesus for his daily salvation from the power of sin, and assures him that the day is coming, for certain, when he will be saved from the presence of sin by being taken into God's immediate presence, where sin can have no place.

Is it arrogance for the man in Christ Jesus to say that he is saved? Is it not humility to say that he is not quite sure? Well, the Bible says that he is saved. He should confess it aloud, to the glory of God. When a believer confesses his salvation from sin and its consequences, he is exalting Jesus the Saviour. All saved people must announce and live out their salvation. Great is their standing.

ADOPTION

A freed slave does need a new status. Christ's death on the cross also made provision for that. The process is called adoption, by which the full rights of a son are conferred upon someone who is not one's son by natural birth. By natural birth, we are the devil's children and bound by him. By His death on the cross, Jesus freed us from that bondage and made us God's adopted sons. Believers are destined to sonship. The Bible says,

> "*For those whom he foreknew he also predestined to be conformed to the image of his Son, in order that he might be the first-born among many brethren*" (Romans 8:29).

> "*For it was fitting that he, for whom and by whom all things exist, in bringing many sons to glory, should make the pioneer of their salvation perfect through suffering. For he who sanctifies and those who are sanctified have all one origin. That is why he is not*

ashamed to call them brethren, saying, 'I will proclaim thy name to
my brethren, in the midst of the congregation I will praise thee.'
And again, 'I will put my trust in Him.' And again, 'Here am I,
and the children God has given me.' Since therefore the children
share in flesh and blood, he himself likewise partook of the same
nature, that through death he might destroy him who has the
power of death, that is, the devil, and deliver all those who
through fear of death were subject to lifelong bondage. For surely
it is not with angels that he is concerned but with the descendants
of Abraham. Therefore he had to be made like his brethren in
every respect, so that he might become a merciful and faithful high
priest in the service of God, to make expiation for the sins of the
people" (Hebrews 2:10-17).

All believers are God's adopted children. They are brothers to Jesus
who is the only begotten Son.

As adopted sons, believers are the objects of the Father's love. The
Lord Jesus prayed, saying,

"I in them and thou in me, that they may become perfectly one, so that
the world may know that thou hast sent me and hast loved them
even as thou hast loved me" (John 17:23).

As adopted sons, believers bear God's image (II Peter 1:4), and are
indwelt by His Spirit,

"... so that we might receive adoption as sons. And because you are
sons, God has sent the Spirit of his Son into our hearts, crying,
'Abba! Father!' " (Galatians 4:5-6).

Adopted sons are also heirs of God and co-heirs with Christ (Romans
8:17; I Peter 1:4).

By Christ's death on the cross, this possibility of becoming God's
children is open to everyone in general and to you in particular. You
can indeed become a child of God and enjoy all the privileges of a

son, even to the extent of sharing the throne of God with the Lord
Jesus.

> *"But to all who received him, who believed in his name, he gave
> power to become children of God"* (John 1:12).

HEAVENLY CITIZENSHIP

The new birth is carried out from above. It is something carried out
by God. At the moment of conversion, God puts something in the
one to whom He imparts new life that is essentially of the other
world. The Lord Jesus said,

> *"My kingship is not of this world"* (John 18:36).

Because Jesus, the first Son, is other-worldly, all true believers are
other-worldly. The Lord Jesus testified to them, saying,

> "They are not of the world, even as I am not of the world"
> (John 17:14).

Believers are citizens of heaven. The Bible says,

> "For here we have no lasting city, but we seek the city which is
> to come" (Hebrews 13:14).

> *"But our commonwealth is in heaven, and from it we await a
> Saviour, the Lord Jesus Christ"* (Philippians 3:20).

The Lord Jesus said,

> *"In my Father's house are many rooms; if it were not so, would I have
> told you that I go to prepare a place for you? And when I go and
> prepare a place for you, I will come again and will take you to
> myself, that where I am you may be also"* (John 14:2-3).

You, believer, are heaven's ambassador to earth with full diplomatic status.

You might be wondering how an unworthy person like you can receive the full rights of heaven. You may feel that you do not deserve it. This feeling is right, for you, by nature as a sinner, deserve nothing but the lake of fire. However, you have been rendered worthy by the death and resurrection of Jesus on your behalf. Let me illustrate it this way, by a true story. Many years ago, in the colonial era when every white person was considered to be a dignitary, an important football match was to take place in Kampala, Uganda. All dignitaries were invited. A certain missionary, as a white dignitary, was also invited and given a special V.I.P pass to the football match. However, owing to pressing duties, he gave his V.I.P pass to one of his primary school teachers, and asked him to attend the football match on his behalf. When the teacher got to the stadium, by the looks of his unimpressive clothing, he was asked to go away from the V.I.P entrance. He insisted that he had a pass to the match, and so the police thought that if a man like him had a ticket, it must be for the open stand. So they asked him to go to the open stand. On his way to that stand, he met another policeman who did not look at his appearance but at his ticket. On seeing that he had a special V.I.P pass, he said to him, "You are for that comfortable stand there. Your ticket indicates that." So this poorly dressed man went to the V.I.P stand, and as he showed his ticket to the police officers in attendance, they saluted him and asked him to go even further until he got to the most important seats and was ushered to a seat. He then found to his utter amazement that he was sitting next to the famous king of Buganda and the colonial governor of Uganda. On his own merit he deserved nothing, but by virtue of the pass that was undeservedly given to him, he was given a place of the highest honour.

At the moment that you, a lost sinner, receive Christ as your personal Saviour, even though you have no merits of your own, God, however, confers upon you spiritual greatness. He gives you heavenly citizenship free of charge, makes you His ambassador on earth with special diplomatic status and duties, as well as very special diplomatic immunity. In addition to all these, at death or at the return of Christ, you will be given a special V.I.P pass to all the important banquets in heaven. Angels will stand by to salute you and direct you to the seat of greatest honour - the throne of God - and there you will reign and feast with Christ!

These are the far-reaching privileges of the new creation. These privileges are found in union with Christ and with Christ alone. Outside of Him there is nothing but doom. We proclaim Christ and the benefits found in Him. How great they are! How far-reaching! What a wonderful Gospel to proclaim!

QUESTIONS

1. What is the meaning of the statement, "Christ is the second Adam"?
2. What is the difference between conversion and reformation?
3. How can we know from the Bible that God is able to impart new life?
4. How long does it take for God to save a sinner?
5. Why will the Lord Jesus not save anyone who comes to Him half-heartedly?
6. What is repentance?
7. When did you repent?
8. Is repentance enough for a sinner to be saved? Explain your answer.
9. How can a sinner receive the Lord Jesus?
10. When did you personally receive the Lord Jesus?
11. Give two marks of a truly saved person.
12. Explain briefly what is meant by justification.
13. What part has Jesus to play in the justification of a sinner?
14. Try on your own to illustrate justification.
15. What is redemption?
16. What did the Lord Jesus do in order to redeem sinners?
17. What is reconciliation?
18. How did Jesus reconcile sinners to God?

19. Is there anyone to whom you need to be reconciled? What will you do about it?

20. What does it mean to be "born again"?

21. Why must a man be born again?

22. Briefly explain how you received the power to become a child of God.

23. Is it not alright if a person knows all about the new birth and can explain it properly, even if he himself has never experienced it?

24. Can a person know for certain that he is saved while he is still in this world?

25. Are you saved?

26. Are you being saved?

27. Will you be saved?

28. Are all human beings the sons of God? Explain clearly.

29. What is adoption?

30. How can a lost sinner become a "Brother" to the Lord Jesus?

31. How can someone who is a Cameroonian citizen also become a citizen of heaven?

32. What rights and privileges do you enjoy as a citizen of heaven?

33. Memorize the following verses:

34. 2 Corinthians 5:17

35. John 1:12-13

36. Ephesians 2:8-9.

5

TERMINATING WITH THE PAST

Therefore, if any one is in Christ, he is a new creation; the old has passed away, behold, the new has come" (II Corinthians 5:17).

When a person receives the Lord Jesus as his Lord and Saviour, the Lord forgives him all his sins and blots away all that stood against him in the heavenly record. However, for him to grow properly in the new life, he must deliberately co-operate with God by terminating with his past life.

TERMINATING WITH RELATIONSHIPS WITH THE SUPERNATURAL

The supernatural realm is in two dimensions: the supernatural that relates to God who is the Father of our Lord and Saviour Jesus Christ, and the supernatural which relates to the devil and all his principalities and powers. The supernatural dealing with God is to be encouraged and the supernatural dealing with the devil is to be terminated with.

Young convert, before you received the Lord, you might have had the following contacts with forbidden supernatural practices:

1. Practice of magic.

2. Contact with sorcerers in one form or the other.
3. Contact with the dead and the worship of ancestors.
4. Attempts to foretell the future through astrology, horoscope, palmistry, mediums, fortune-tellers, and so on.
5. Contact with mystical secret societies of local origin like the Ogboni society, Famla, Nyamkwe, Obassinjom, Ngondo, and so on.
6. Contact with mystical secret societies of foreign origin like the rosicrucian order (ARMOC), free-masonry, yoga, transcendental meditation, lodges, and so on.
7. Talismans and all that is used for personal protection.
8. Charms and all that is used to influence others, e.g, love potions used to seduce and maintain the love of others.
9. Brain pills and all that is used to acquire intelligence or examination success.
10. The use of magical powers for success in football and other games.

You must break with them at once. The life of God in you through the Lord Jesus is so entirely opposed to these supernatural activities of the devil that you cannot continue in them as a child of God. In the past, while you were a child of the devil, you could continue in these practices that originated with your father the devil. Now that you have changed parentage, you have also changed kingdoms. You must leave all that belongs to the kingdom which you have abandoned.

God is opposed to these practices. He says,

"You shall not practise augury or witchcraft ... You shall not make any cuttings in your flesh on account of the dead or tattoo any marks upon you: I am the Lord" (Leviticus 19:26-28).

"Do not turn to mediums or wizards; do not seek them out, to be defiled by them: I am the Lord your God" (Leviticus 19:31).

"There shall not be found among you any one who burns his son or his daughter as an offering, any one who practises divination, a soothsayer, or an augur, or a sorcerer, or a charmer, or a medium, or a wizard, or a necromancer. For whoever does these things is an abomination to the Lord" (Deuteronomy 18:10-12).

God punishes all who have dealings with such things. His Word says,

"You shall not permit a sorceress to live" (Exodus 22:18).

"If a person turns to mediums and wizards, playing the harlot after them, I will set my face against that person and will cut him off from among his people" (Leviticus 20:6).

"A man or a woman who is a medium or a wizard shall be put to death" (Leviticus 20:27).

"But as for... sorcerers ... their lot shall be in the lake that burns with fire and sulphur, which is the second death" (Revelation 21:8).

You are not to break with them because they are impotent. No. Sometimes they have great power. Sometimes their revelations are true and their predictions correct. Sometimes their knowledge is true. The problem is not whether or not they are true. The crucial question is, "What is their origin? Whom do they serve? Do they offer only temporary help or do they offer eternal help?"

All these practices use the power of the devil. The devil is their originator. He gives them a beginning and sustains them. For that reason, all that comes from them is to be rejected, even if it appears helpful. In Philippi, there was a slave girl with a spirit of divination that brought her owners great gain by soothsaying. The spirit even recognized Paul and Silas and spoke out what was true about them, saying,

"These men are servants of the Most High God, who proclaim to you the way of salvation" (Acts 16:17).

What was being said was true, but the source was from the devil. Paul could have allowed it in the hope that her pronouncements would help people to believe him and his message. He could have said, "It is the truth. It will help, irrespective of the source." Of course he knew that the source, being the devil, could never help God. Nothing from the devil can help God. All healings by sorcerers, witch doctors, ... are from the devil's kingdom. You should not just ask, "Is this good or bad? Is it profitable or unprofitable?" You must ask, "Is it of God or of Satan?" Satan may offer things that appear good. They are all to be rejected. God may offer things that may appear bad. They are all to be received with thanksgiving. So Paul turned and said to the spirit,

> "'I charge you in the name of Jesus Christ to come out of her.' And it
> came out that very hour" (Acts 16:18).

Paul perhaps knew that such an action would bring them trouble, but nevertheless he did it. He was not out to compromise. True servants of the Lord proclaim and practise the whole truth at any price. He did not say, "Let me leave the girl alone so that my ministry may not have complications." No! He cast out the spirit and got imprisonment as a well earned 'thank you '. The only way to further the Kingdom of God is to denounce all the works of the devil. Please put an end to all of them.

THE EPHESIAN EXAMPLE

The Bible says about the Ephesian believers,

> "Many also of those who were now believers came, confessing and
> divulging their practices. And a number of those who practised
> magic arts brought their books together and burned them in the
> sight of all; and they counted the value of them and found it came
> to fifty thousand pieces of silver. So the word of the Lord grew and
> prevailed mightily" (Acts 19:18-20).

We can learn the following from these believers:

1. They did not hide the deeds of darkness in which they were involved prior to their conversion to Christ. They exposed them and confessed them.
2. They destroyed everything that had to do with their sinful past, expensive as that was.
3. These things were destroyed (burnt) publicly and not thrown away privately.
4. This action resulted in spiritual growth for the work of the Lord.

You must not hide magical activities in which you were once involved. Expose them and confess them. Bring all these things to the assembly of God's children so that they should be destroyed, regardless of what they cost you. In this way, you will contribute to the growth of the Gospel. You have no choice about this.

IDOLATRY

In the first and second commandments, God said to man,

> "You shall have no other gods besides me. You shall not make for yourself a graven image, or any likeness of anything that is in heaven above, or that is in the earth beneath or that is in the water under the earth; you shall not bow down to them or serve them" (Exodus 20:3-5).

Idolatry includes having any person, thing, system, philosophy on the throne of the heart above, besides or next to God. God must have the first place in an absolute sense. It also includes the making of any images of God or man or anything to represent God. It includes the bowing to objects, the making and keeping of pictures of "Jesus," and the like. All this is idolatry.

If you set yourself up to the place in life where you are prepared to do what you think or like or want, instead of what God wants, you should know that you are an idolater. Anyone who deliberately sins, that is, he deliberately does what he knows that God does not want, has raised himself to the place of final authority and is, unquestionably, an idolater.

If your job, ambitions, education, wife (or husband), children, parents, government, girlfriend (or boyfriend) or any other thing takes the first place in your life, you are an idolater. To know if you are worshipping a thing or not can be tested very easily by the following simple tests:

1. Has God asked me not to have this thing? If you still keep it after the Lord has asked you to get rid of it, then you are worshipping it.
2. Does this thing hinder my walk with God in any way? If it hinders your walk with God and you still keep it, you are worshipping it.
3. Am I prepared to let it go any moment that the Lord asks me to let it go? If you are hesitant or unwilling, you are worshipping it.

All that you are worshipping are idols. You must put an end to them! Images, statues, ... of God or Jesus or Mary or any other "saint", bones from "saints" being kept for their magical healing powers, other wooden, metal or stone images, must be destroyed. You cannot bow to the image of Jesus and also bow to Jesus. All who bow to images or make, keep, distribute and sell them are enemies of the Lord Jesus. All knees are to bow to Jesus alone.

The supposed pictures of Jesus or any other personality in the Bible, are the devil's lies. No pictures were taken of anyone in the Bible. The pictures that are said to be the pictures of Jesus are the products of minds that are at enmity with God. What of saints as intermediaries? What of saints praying for us? What of Holy Mary praying for us? These are all the devil's lies. There is one God and only one intermediary between God and man - Jesus. All other intermediaries are abominations to God.

"For there is one God, and there is one mediator between God and men, the man Christ Jesus, who gave himself as a ransom for all,

the testimony to which was borne at the proper time" (1 Timothy 2:5-6).

"How much more shall the blood of Christ, who through the eternal Spirit offered himself without blemish to God, purify your conscience from dead works to serve the living God. Therefore he (Jesus Christ) is the mediator of a new covenant, so that those who are called may receive the promised eternal inheritance, since a death has occurred which redeems them from the transgressions under the first covenant" (Hebrews 9:14-15).

All that is carried out, even in the name of the Lord Jesus, by men who worship religious idols and have other intermediaries apart from Jesus, is dead works. When they repent from dead works and come to the Lord Jesus and to Him alone, they will be redeemed by the Lord Jesus. You cannot be redeemed by Jesus and be redeemed by Holy Mary.

GETTING RID OF IDOLS

All idols must be gotten rid of, so that the idol-worshipper can turn to the Lord in spirit and in truth and worship Him as He deserves to be worshipped. The Bible says, "But the hour is coming, and now is, when the true worshippers will worship the Father in spirit and in truth, for such the Father seeks to worship him." God is spirit and not a statue, not an image. He is to be worshipped in spirit and in truth, and not by rosaries and lies. How do we get rid of idols? Let us learn from the example of Gideon.

Gideon was called by the Lord. He knew God. God planned to use him, but before God could use him for other purposes, God had to use him to pull down idols. The Bible says,

"That night the Lord said to him, 'Take your father's bull, the second bull seven years old, and pull down the altar of Baal which your father has, and cut down the Asherah that is beside it; and build an altar to the Lord your God on the top of the stronghold here,

> *with stones laid in due order; then take the second bull, and offer it*
> *as a burnt offering with the wood of the Asherah which you shall*
> *cut down.' So Gideon took ten men of his servants, and did as the*
> *Lord had told him" (Judges 6:25-27).*

How did the people react? They wanted to kill him (Judges 6:30). How did God react to it? The Bible says,

> *"But the Spirit of the Lord took possession of Gideon" (Judges 6:34).*

You, too, must do the same. Break down and destroy all idols. Then offer a sacrifice of your life to the Lord. He will receive it and, in return, He will let His Spirit possess you. Will you be a Gideon today? What is God asking you to part with? What is God asking you to break down? Will you obey?

REJECTING THE INFLUENCE OF SATANIC POWERS

You may have been brought up in an atmosphere where the devil was worshipped in one way or the other. One member or the other of your family, especially your parents, may have been or are involved in witchcraft or with satanic powers in one way or the other. By their action, you are passively involved. You may have been dedicated to the devil or been baptized into Satan. A sorcerer or astrologer may have been consulted on your behalf. You are, therefore, not free.

To get free from these entanglements, I suggest that you confess your own sins in this area and also the sins of your parents or relatives in this area of life. Then, actively, by calling upon the name of the Lord Jesus, break all the bonds - strong or weak - that bind you to your family as far as those supernatural involvements are concerned, and take your stand out of that family and into the family of God. Tell the devil that from that moment his power over you, as a result of such activities, is broken for ever. Tell him that by your act now of breaking with your parents' supernatural involvement and taking cover under the blood of Jesus, you have no part in all the activities that your parents may carry out in your name from now on and forever. By that act of breaking with the past, you stand totally free in the Lord Jesus.

DO NOT FEAR

You may be afraid to throw away all the rings, charms,... and to break down all the idols that you know you should break down, for fear that the devil will react. Indeed, he will surely react, but nevertheless, do not fear. The Lord Jesus who lives in you, is stronger than the devil. The Bible says,

> *"Little children, you are of God, and have overcome them; for he who is in you is greater than he who is in the world"* (I John 4:4).

The Lord Jesus said,

> *"Behold, I have given you authority to tread upon serpents and scorpions, and over all the power of the enemy; and nothing shall hurt you"* (Luke 10:19).

All the power of hell is impotent against you as you stand fully protected in Christ. Maybe what you fear is physical death or suffering that will result from your destruction of idols that must be destroyed. Do not fear. The Lord Jesus said,

> *"And do not fear those who kill the body but cannot kill the soul; rather fear him who can destroy both soul and body in hell"* (Matthew 10:28).

Also bear in mind that even as far as your physical life is concerned, no harm can come to you without the permission of your heavenly Father. All that He permits will ultimately result in a blessing for you. Pilate said to Jesus,

> *"'Do you not know that I have power to release you, and power to crucify you?' Jesus answered him, 'You would have no power over*

me unless it had been given you from above; therefore he who delivered me to you has the greater sin'" (John 19:10-11).

You, too, should rest assured that no one can have power over you unless he is allowed from heaven, and what God allows will turn out for your ultimate good. Look to Jesus. Have eternity in view. Fear God and do what He wants. Say to yourself, "The Lord is for me, who can be against me and succeed?"

TERMINATING WITH PAST SEXUAL RELATIONSHIPS

Before you knew the Lord you may have had boyfriends (or girl-friends), men or women in your life who were not your legal partners. You may have been keeping a woman as a concubine. You may have had a steady sex partner or several sex partners. You may have been masturbating or involved in homosexual practices in one form or the other.

You may have been reading dirty novels or involved in questionable petting. You may have been engaged to or hoping to be engaged to an unbeliever. You may have continued to have some sexual relationship with the father or mother of your illegitimate child or children. You may have had special delight in pornography. You are to stop all such practices. You are to break with all such relationships and you are to break with them at once.

The Bible says

> *"Do you not know that the unrighteous will not inherit the kingdom of God? Do not be deceived; neither fornicators, nor idolaters, nor adulterers, nor sexual perverts, nor thieves, nor the greedy, nor drunkards, nor revilers, nor robbers will inherit the kingdom of God. And such were some of you. But you were washed, you were sanctified, you were justified in the name of the Lord Jesus Christ and in the Spirit of our God"* (1 Corinthians 6:9-11).

Again the Word of God says,

"Do not be mismated with unbelievers. For what partnership have righteousness and iniquity? Or what fellowship has light with darkness? What accord has Christ with Belial? Or what has a believer in common with an unbeliever? What agreement has the temple of God with idols? For we are the temple of the living God; as God said, 'I will live in them and move among them, and I will be their God, and they shall be my people. Therefore come out from them, and be separate from them,' says the Lord, 'and touch nothing unclean; then I will welcome you, and I will be a Father to you, and you shall be my sons and daughters, says the Lord Almighty'" (II Corinthians 6:14-18).

You, as a believer, cannot marry an unbeliever! The unbeliever belongs to the devil. You belong to God. The devil cannot be married to God. There is an eternal divorce between the two. You may be engaged to an unbeliever, but let me tell you that your conversion has brought that engagement to an end. You are the temple of God. How can you continue in an engagement with someone who is the temple of the devil? You are clean. The unbeliever is unclean. The Bible says, "Touch not the unclean thing."

You may be haunted by past sexual relationships. The devil may bring to your memory past sexual relationships in order to turn your face back to things that you have abandoned. Reject his suggestions. Take hold of your authority in the name of the Lord Jesus and reject all the ties that link you to your sinful past. Break the power of all sexual sins in the name of Jesus, and you will find that you are delivered completely. If there is an unbeliever in your life who does not want to leave you, pray in this fashion:

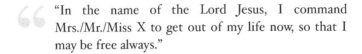

"In the name of the Lord Jesus, I command Mrs./Mr./Miss X to get out of my life now, so that I may be free always."

As you take that stand in prayer and refuse all co-operation with the devil, you will experience victory and deliverance. God bless you!

One thing that will help you to break any ties with undesirable people, is to return anything that they gave you as part of the price for using you. If the man gave you money, household goods, musical equipment, etc, as part of the price for using you, then when you receive the Lord Jesus, you must return his property. If you do not do so, those things will remind you of the wicked past and the devil will continue to torment you. It is costly, but your total freedom in Christ is far more important than all that you may part with. Another reason why you must return all proceeds from sinful relationships is that, unless you do so, you have no testimony before that person. He will not take your conversion seriously until you have returned the price that he paid for your body! If you received goods which are now lost or have become old from use, you should calculate the equivalent and pay that person in cash. This is the way of the new life. Finally, you should stop seeing that person. Do not say, "I want to go and see him in order to witness to him." Introduce him to another believer who should then try to reach him for Christ. If you attempt to reach him yourself, you may find yourself in fresh entanglements.

TERMINATING WITH PROFESSIONS THAT DISHONOUR CHRIST

If before your conversion you worked for a tobacco company, you must stop working for that company. It is not God's will that people should destroy themselves by smoking. Your body is the temple of the Holy Spirit (I Corinthians 6:19). You must not destroy God's temple with smoking and the accompanying diseases. If you do, God will destroy you (1 Corinthians 3:16-17). Tobacco is bad for you and for all the creatures of God. You must not contribute in any way towards its production or use. So, stop smoking at once. Stop giving cigarettes to people. Stop selling cigarettes and stop working for a cigarette production company. Ask God for a new occupation that honours Him. The same applies to alcohol. The Bible says,

"*Wine is a mocker, strong drink a brawler; and whoever is led astray by it is not wise*" (Proverbs 20:1).

Stop drinking alcohol. Stop serving alcohol. Stop helping the production of alcohol in any way. The Bible says that no drunkard will inherit the Kingdom of God (1 Corinthians 6:10). No one is born a drunkard. You may give a man the first glass of drink that will lead him on the way of ruin as a drunkard and, finally, to hell. Dare you do that? So, do not drink alcohol. Do not go to bars and drinking houses. They are the devil's workshops for destroying health, life, family and the nation.

Do not go to night clubs. They are places frequented by empty men and women who have lost their sense of direction in life. They are also the devil's workshops. If you were working in a night club, please terminate with it. That is not the place for you. Do not go to watch worldly films. Imagine all the bloodshed, immorality and crime that is displayed on the screen. Is that what you want to fill your mind with? Certainly not. So, do not go there. Do not help anyone to go there. Do not work there.

As you terminate with these unfruitful works of darkness, you should trust the Lord to help you to find the job that He has in store for you, where you can truly serve Him. You need a job. He will supply all your needs. The Bible says,

> *"Have no anxiety about anything, but in everything by prayer and supplication with thanksgiving let your requests be made known to God. And the peace of God, which passes all understanding, will keep your hearts and your minds in Christ Jesus"* (Philippians 4:6-7).

Furthermore, the Word of God says,

> "And my God will supply every need of yours according to his riches in glory in Christ Jesus" (Philippians 4:19).

TERMINATING WITH UNHEALTHY FAMILY TIES

You belonged to an earthly family before conversion. At conversion you were born into the family of God. Your first loyalty must now be to the Lord and His family. This does not mean that you stop being helpful to your family members. It simply means that your ultimate loyalty is elsewhere. In practice, this means that if the demands of your husband, wife, children, parents, ... conflict with the demands of the Lord Jesus, you will go ahead at once and obey the Lord Jesus. There must be no question about this at all. It is Jesus first. The Bible says,

> "Now great multitudes accompanied him; and he turned and said to them, 'If any one comes to me and does not hate his own father and mother and wife and children and brothers and sisters, yes, and even his own life, he cannot be my disciple'" (Luke 14:25-26).

Jesus said,

> "Do not think that I have come to bring peace on earth; I have not come to bring peace, but a sword. For I have come to set a man against his father, and a daughter against her mother, and a daughter-in-law against her mother-in-law; and a man's foes will be those of his own household. He who loves father or mother more than me is not worthy of me; and he who loves son or daughter more than me is not worthy of me" (Matthew 10:34-37).

Love your family, but let your final loyalty be to the Lord Jesus and the household of God.

The proverb says, "Like father, like son." We tend to carry with us family character traits. Some of these are assets and others are liabilities. Some family traits which children take over from their parents and which are liabilities include: laziness, indiscipline, gluttony, restlessness, temper, untidiness, ... You should break with these character flaws that you took over from your parents or the people in whose environment you were brought up. Claim the power of the Lord Jesus and be delivered from all these.

There are also hereditary traits like baldness, early grey hair, sickle cell anaemia, ... which are inherited from parents without any personal choice whatsoever. One should break with all these in the name of Jesus. The Bible says, "But he was wounded for our transgressions, he was bruised for our iniquities; upon him was the chastisement that made us whole, and with his stripes we are healed" (Isaiah 53:5). When the Lord Jesus went to the cross, He took all our sicknesses and diseases, as well as all our infirmities with Him and nailed them to His cross. He took sickle cell anaemia genes, as well as all the other undesirable genes, with Him to the cross. We can be free from all these. This is part of our inheritance. We should also claim our healing from all diseases and deformities in the name of Jesus. Perfect health and perfect form are yours in the Lord Jesus.

TERMINATING WITH CHRISTLESS SOCIAL TRADITIONS

There are social traditions that bind people and enslave them. Some of these include expensive birth celebrations, death celebrations, the offering of libations at parties, These are purely worldly traditions and are unhelpful. You are not to indulge in them. Keep yourself pure for the Lord. Be free to serve Him and to serve Him alone.

PRINCIPLES OF CONDUCT

To help you to decide whether or not to carry out a certain practice, ask yourself the following questions:

1. Who is the author of this? Is it God or Satan? If God is the Author, then there is the possibility that you can do it.
2. Who will this action glorify? Is it God or Satan or self? Do not do it, if it will glorify Satan or self.
3. Will it help me to grow in Christ or will it retard me?
4. Only do what will help you to grow.
5. Will it put me in conditions where I may be tempted?
6. If so, keep away from it.
7. Will it help others to see Christ in me? If not, do not do it; for you are an ambassador for Christ.
8. Will others do the same thing and perhaps fall into sin, even though you can do it without falling into sin? If the activity is

likely to cause a young believer to fall, then, out of love for him, do not do it.

9. Will it lead to a habit from which I may not easily set myself free? If so, do not do it.

10. Is it the right time for it? Something may be right when done at a particular time, but wrong at a different time. There is a time for everything (Ecclesiastes 3:1 - 8).

Finally, the Holy Spirit will guide you. Look up to Him. The Lord Jesus said,

"*When the Spirit of truth comes, he will guide you into all the truth*" (John 16:13).

QUESTIONS

In what two dimensions does the supernatural exist?

1. In which dimension of the supernatural must the believer not be involved?

2. Can the supernatural life of God co-exist with the supernatural activity of the devil in the same person?

3. In what supernatural activities of the devil were you introduced before you received the Lord Jesus as your Saviour and Lord?

4. Have you broken with these supernatural contacts with the devil? If your answer is, "Yes," explain when and how you broke with these supernatural contacts.

5. What are the consequences of continued contact with the devil's supernatural?

6. What are the benefits to the Gospel that result from a public termination with the supernatural contacts with Satan?

7. Who is an idolater?

8. What were the idols in your life before you received the Lord Jesus as your Saviour?

9. Have these idols been destroyed since you believed? If your answer is, "Yes," explain when and how you destroyed them.

10. Who alone deserves human worship and adoration?

11. What must be done to images, idols, pictures of the "Lord Jesus" and the "saints."?

12. How many mediators has God established between man and Himself?

13. Is there anything wrong in man establishing more mediators than God has allowed?

14. How did Gideon satisfy the heart of God and was, thereby, called to further service?

15. Was Gideon congratulated by the public for destroying the idols of his father?

16. What blessings come with the destruction of the idols in any life?

17. Are your parents or relatives involved with the Satanic supernatural in any way?

18. If they are so involved, what must you do to break yourself from all that may link you to these powers because of their activities?

19. Why is the devil powerless over the child of God who has destroyed all the idols in his life?

20. Whom should a child of God fear and why?

21. Were you involved in unrighteous sexual relationships before you received Christ?

22. What particular relationships were you involved in and what must you do to put an end to them now that you are a child of God?

23. On what date did you or will you actually put those relationships to an end?

24. Why can you not continue in these relationships, now that you have believed, since some of them brought you some gain?

25. Were you involved in a sexual relationship before you believed which still haunts you, even though you have believed and broken with it?

26. Now that you are a child of God, what criteria will you take into consideration in deciding whether or not you should keep your job?

27. You are a child of two families. Which are these?
28. Where should your prior loyalty be?
29. Why must the Lord Jesus take the first place in your heart?
30. Who are likely to be your greatest enemies as a child of God?
31. Are you facing persecution from your family because of your faith in the Lord? Is this a normal reaction that you should expect or is it very strange?
32. What physical or character liabilities have you inherited from your human family?
33. Is there provision in the Lord Jesus for breaking with these? Which is the provision?
34. Have you made use of that provision?
35. Memorize the following verses: Exodus 20:3-5; 1 Timothy 2:5-6; Luke 10:26-27; 2 Corinthians 6:14-18; Isaiah 53:5-6.

6

ASSURANCE OF SALVATION

THE NEED FOR FULL ASSURANCE

It is God's will that all who have been made into new creatures through union with the Lord Jesus in His death, resurrection and exaltation should know for certain that they have eternal life and, therefore, will never perish. This assurance that they have permanently passed from death unto life in Christ, that the Lord will surely keep them to the end, that because they are in Christ they will be in heaven, is the right of the true believer, and he ought to enter into his full inheritance.

This knowledge of the assurance that the Lord will keep the true believer until the end is important for the following reasons:

1. It leads to rest in the Lord. Without the assurance of salvation, there is no rest in the Lord. A believer who has no assurance of salvation continues to strive in the energy of the flesh to please God so as to be saved some day. His service for the Lord is not out of the joy of salvation, but out of the fear that he may be cast away. Their commitment is out of the fear that they may be cast away. Such cannot truly love the Lord; for perfect love casts out fear. With assurance of salvation, God's new creation sets out to please the Lord out

of gratitude for so complete but unmerited salvation. Such service is pure and flows freely. If a woman is married to a man whom she fears may divorce her some day, she can never be totally at peace in that home. Jesus calls His children to rest and to peace. He says, *"Peace I leave with you; my peace I give to you; not as the world gives do I give to you. Let not your hearts be troubled, neither let them be afraid"* (John 14:27).

2. It leads to total commitment to the Lord. When a believer knows that he belongs to the Lord Jesus now and will belong to Him throughout all time and all eternity, he will give his all to the Lord Jesus, out of gratitude. He will serve Him more fully and without any reservation whatsoever. Again, think of a woman who knows for certain that her marriage will stand the tests of time and trials. Such a woman will give her all to her husband and serve him more devotedly. On the other hand, the woman who is afraid that some day, through some fault on her part, she could be sent away from the marriage, will never give her all to the man and will never put her all into the relationship. She will keep something back, so that if the marriage ever breaks, she will not be completely broken but can start all over again.

3. Jesus has promised to keep His own to the end. Not to know this or, worse, to doubt Him, is to sin deeply.

THE NEED FOR TRUE CONVERSION

Before we consider in detail the full assurance of salvation that is found in the Lord Jesus, we want to make it clear that what we are going to say here does not apply to everybody. There are false conversions! There are many who make some confession of faith and even seem to show some apparent evidence of the presence of the Holy Spirit in their lives, but who are not truly born again. To assure such of eternal security in the Lord Jesus, would be a drastic lie, because they are not at all in the Lord Jesus.

Of the four soils on which the sower's seeds fell, three were useless for God. The seed on the road never germinated at all. That was never truly good soil. It was useless soil. That on the stony ground germinated and for some time seemed to be going on but, it, too, died off to show that it was never really true. That which fell amongst thorns was choked. It never produced. It, too, was not genuine. That which was on good soil bore fruit. That alone represents genuine conversion.

We state very categorically that this message on assurance applies only to those who are the good soil. These hear the Word, accept it and bear fruit (Mark 4:20). Human beings might have mistaken the stony soil and thorny soil for good soil, but God makes no mistakes.

"The Lord knows those who are his" (II Timothy 2:19).

So full assurance is for those who are genuine; those who are known by the Lord as His. Such people make a total response to the Lord with their wills, minds (understanding) and affections (emotions). Many people are committed in their wills and emotions, but they do not understand, and so they cannot go far. Others are committed in their understanding and emotions, but their wills are not committed, and so they do not go far. Others still are committed in their understanding and wills, but their emotions are not committed, so they fail.

Let us look at three classic examples from the Word of God:

THE RICH YOUNG RULER (MARK 10:17-22)

1. His emotions were committed. He fell at the feet of Jesus and worshipped Him.
2. His understanding (will) was committed. He knew what the law said and knew that something more had to be done. That is why he came to the Lord.
3. His will was not committed. Jesus knew this and He made a demand of him that was aimed at having his will committed. He said to him, *"You lack one thing; go, sell what you have, and give to the poor, and you will have treasure in heaven; and come, follow me"* (Mark 10:21). Was his will involved in his decision

to have eternal life? Was he willing? No. He was not willing.
He understood well. He had the right feelings, but *"At that
saying his countenance fell, and he went away sorrowful; for he had
great possessions"* (Mark 10:22). Many modern evangelists
would have welcomed him into the "Kingdom." They would
have assured him of salvation, although he was not saved.
Many pastors would have later on called him a backslider.
However, he had never been saved. He had never slid
forward into the Kingdom. May I ask you a question: "Is
your will involved in your commitment?" If not, you are not a
child of God. If you are not prepared to obey Jesus in all the
details of your life now, you do not belong to Him. Again,
may I ask you, "Is your will committed?"

THE SCRIBE

> *"And a Scribe came up and said to him, 'Teacher, I will follow you
> wherever you go.' And Jesus said to him, 'Foxes have holes, and
> birds of the air have nests; but the Son of man has nowhere to lay
> his head' "... (Matthew 8:19-20).*

1. His will was committed. He wanted to follow Jesus
   everywhere.
2. His affections were committed.
3. His understanding was not committed. Therefore, Jesus said
   to him, "I have no home. If you follow Me, you, too, will
   have no home. I have no visible means of support. If you
   follow Me, you, too, will have no visible means of support."
   He had to understand what it would cost. Did he understand
   it?

THE DISCIPLE

> "Another of the disciples said to him, 'Lord, let me first go and
> bury my father.' But Jesus said to him, 'Follow me, and
> leave the dead to bury their own dead' "(Matthew 8:21-22).

1. His will was committed.
2. His understanding was committed, clear.
3. His affections were not committed. They were entangled.
   Part of him yearned for Jesus and part yearned for his
   parents. Jesus was saying to him, "Your emotions are
   confused. Sort them out. Is it Me you want or your parents?
   If you want Me, let the dead bury their own dead."

So, as you see, Jesus demanded total commitment from all those who
would follow Him. He accepted no half-measures. He coaxed nobody.
He begged no one to come. He invited all who would come to Him
to count the cost! Because the Lord knows human beings, He is not
moved by crowds. He is not moved by mere tears. He looks deeper.
The Bible says,

> "Now when he was in Jerusalem at the Passover feast, many believed
> in his name when they saw the signs which he did; BUT JESUS
> DID NOT COMMIT HIMSELF TO THEM BECAUSE HE
> KNEW ALL MEN AND NEEDED NO ONE TO BEAR
> WITNESS OF MAN; FOR HE HIMSELF KNEW WHAT
> WAS IN MAN" (John 2:23-25).

The Lord considers as saved those who respond to Him with their
wills, understanding and affections. All the others are not saved,
whatever they may profess. If anyone is still deliberately practising
sin, that is, knowing that something is sin and yet going ahead to
carry it out, may he be warned. These are very strong indications that
he is not a child of God. The Bible says,

> "Every one who commits sin is guilty of lawlessness; sin is
> lawlessness. You know that he appeared to take away sins,
> and in him there is no sin. NO ONE who abides in him
> sins; no one who sins has either seen him or known him.
> Little children, let no one deceive you. He who does right
> is righteous, as he is righteous. He who commits sin is of
> the devil; for the devil has sinned from the beginning. The
> reason the Son of God appeared was to destroy the works

of the devil. No one born of God commits sin; for God's nature abides in him, and he cannot sin because he is born of God. By this it may be seen who are the children of God, and who are the children of the devil: whoever does not do right is not of God, nor he who does not love his brother" (1 John 3:4-10).

If you have parted with all known sins and are, by God's grace, living in fellowship with the Lord Jesus, and with your whole heart you are determined to love Him to the end, I assure you on the basis of God's Word that you are eternally secure in the arms of the Lord Jesus. Below are solid reasons from the Word of God on which to base your assurance.

THE FOREKNOWLEDGE OF GOD

You did not become a believer by some accident. God knew from the foundations of the world that you would be born and would receive Christ. He accepted from the very foundations of the world to come and dwell in you. He cannot change His mind in time about decisions that were taken in eternity! He foreknew you with your peculiar weaknesses and failures, yet He ordained that in Christ you would come into a saving knowledge of Him. That foreknowledge and fore-ordination, He has now accomplished in practice by bringing you to a knowledge of His Son. Nothing can destroy God's fore-ordained purpose. The Word of God says,

> *"For those whom he foreknew He also predestined to be conformed to the image of his Son, in order that he might be the first-born among many brethren. And those whom he predestined he also called; and those whom he called he also justified; and those whom he justified he also glorified"* (Romans 8:29-30).

Notice that it is the work of God from start to finish. He foreknew; He predestined; He called; He justified; He glorified. He did not foreknow you as a wonderful person. He foreknew you as a sinner, as a rebel. He did not predestine you because you were wonderful;

rather, He did it because you were helpless. He did not call you because you were very special. His love did it. You stand now in Christ justified, not because of your wonderful spirituality, but because of His unchanging love. He who has done all the rest by His own free choice will surely complete that which He began. He will glorify you when Jesus comes. You should worship Him for so mighty a salvation wrought on your behalf by Him.

The Bible says,

> *"Even as he chose us in him before the foundation of the world, that we should be holy and blameless before him. He destined us in love to be his sons through Jesus Christ, according to the purpose of his will"* (Ephesians 1:4-5).

The apostle Paul talked of his election in the following terms:

> "But when he who had set me apart before I was born, and had called me through his grace, was pleased to reveal his Son to me, in order that I might preach him among the Gentiles, I did not confer with flesh and blood" (Galatians 1:15-16).

The Lord said of Jeremiah,

> "Before I formed you in the womb I knew you, and before you were born I consecrated you; I appointed you a prophet to the nations" (Jeremiah 1:5).

God knew you before you existed as a physical reality and His purpose for you was formed and established then. That purpose was that, by His grace, you might come to a knowledge of His Son, and through Him be saved eternally. That purpose of God will stand; for God's purposes cannot be thwarted (Job 42:2). The devil and all in the world cannot thwart God's purpose of not only justifying you, but also glorifying you. You see, if God wanted to save you and actually give you faith to believe in Christ but could not save you to the finish, He would be a weak God. However, He is not weak. He is able. His Word says

> "Consequently he is able FOR ALL TIME TO SAVE
> THOSE who draw near to God through him, since he
> always lives to make intercession for them" (Hebrews 7:25).

THE GREAT SALVATION OF GOD

You have been saved with a great salvation. While you were yet a sinner, rebellious and hostile to God, He, out of mercy, chose you unto salvation. He says,

> *"You did not choose me but I chose you"* (John 15:16).

He chose you not because of any special merit, but because of His love for you. From the beginning He saved you by grace and not by merit. The Bible says,

> *"For by grace you have been saved through faith; and this is not your own doing, it is the gift of God - not because of works, lest any man should boast"* (Ephesians 2:8-9).

You were saved by grace through faith. The faith was not something that originated in you. It was a gift of God. The one thing that you contributed in your salvation was your sins, and God contributed everything else. If you were saved on the basis of works, then you should have cause to fear that when your works do not measure up to the required specifications, you will be rejected. But thanks to be to God! It all depended on the gift of God to an undeserving sinner - the gift of faith. God does not repent of His gifts. The apostle said,

> "For the gifts and the call of God are irrevocable" (Romans 11:29).

God does not change us partially. He does not only carry on an external work. He changes from inside. He imparts His own nature to the repentant sinner. How can someone who truly bears the nature of God ever perish? No. Your salvation is deep and thorough, and He has given you His Holy Spirit as a guarantee that He will complete the work that He has begun in you. The Bible wants you to be confident of the fact that,

> "*He who began a good work in you will bring it to completion at the day of Jesus Christ*" (Philippians 1:6).

The apostle wants you to be confident of that fact. Are you? If God had not meant to save you to the end, He would not have started at all; for that would have been a terrible waste of time. He knew you just as you are and decided that He would save you right to the end. He has begun with you and in you. He will finish it. Praise the Lord!

THE COMMITMENT OF CHRIST

The Lord Jesus said,

> "*All that the Father gives me will come to me; and him who comes to me I will not cast out*" (John 6:37).

You were given to Christ by the Father. Christ will ensure that He does not lose you. Will the devil not frustrate the purpose of Christ to save you to the end? No. He cannot. He will try, but the Lord Jesus is stronger than him. Jesus said of the disciples,

> "*While I was with them, I kept them in thy name, which thou hast given me; I have guarded them, and none of them is lost but the son of perdition, that the scripture might be fulfilled*" (John 17:12).

Jesus kept all the disciples, including even Peter who denied Him. He could have kept even Judas, had it not been that He let go so that the Scriptures might be fulfilled.

THE SECURE ARMS OF JESUS AND THE FATHER

The Lord Jesus said,

> *"My sheep hear my voice, and I know them, and they follow me; and I*
> *give them eternal life, and they shall never perish, and no one shall*
> *snatch them out of my hand. My Father, who has given them to*
> *me, is greater than all, and no one is able to snatch them out of the*
> *Father's hand" (John 10:27-29).*

You are in Jesus' hand. That is enough security already. To add to it, the hand of Jesus is in the Father's hand. You are doubly secure there. Keep listening to the voice of Jesus and keep following Him, and your security is fully settled.

There, in the hand of Jesus, no one can snatch you. To get at you the person or thing will first have to destroy and overpower the hand of the Father. After that he will have to destroy the hand of Jesus. Only after that can he get at you. Dearest brother, "Is there someone or something that can overpower God and the Lord Jesus?" No! There is no such thing. The Word of God says,

> *"Who shall separate us from the love of Christ? Shall tribulation, or*
> *distress, or persecution, or famine, or nakedness, or peril, or sword?*
> *As it is written, 'For thy sake we are being killed all the day long;*
> *we are regarded as sheep to be slaughtered.' No, in all these things*
> *we are more than conquerors through him who loved us. For I am*
> *sure that neither death, nor life, nor angels, nor principalities, nor*
> *things present, nor things to come, nor powers, nor height, nor*
> *depth, nor anything else in all creation, will be able to separate us*
> *from the love of God in Christ Jesus our Lord" (Romans 8:35-39).*

The apostle said that he was sure. Are you sure? You should be.

Nothing else (not even the devil) will separate you from the love of God which is in Christ Jesus. You are wonderfully secure.

THE FACTS OF ETERNAL LIFE

The apostle John wrote,

> *"And this is the testimony, that God gave us eternal life, and this life is in his Son. He who has the son has life; he who has not the Son of God has not life. I write this to you who believe in the name of the Son of God, that you may know that you have eternal life"* (1 John 5:11-13).

Do you have the Son of God in you? If your answer is, "Yes," then you have eternal life. If your answer is, "No," then you have eternal death. If you have eternal life, it means that you have God's life in full measure. Anything that can end is not eternal life. Eternal life means partly that it has no end in time. If you a child of God could perish, it would mean that what you had was not eternal life. But God has given you eternal life. Be sure that you will always have it in Christ. Know that you have it, and act with the authority of someone who will never perish. God gave His only Son so that you should not perish. If after you have received the Son of God into your heart, you should then go and perish with Him in you, then something would be seriously wrong with God's purpose.

VIII. THE FACT OF THE INDWELLING HOLY SPIRIT

At the moment of conversion, God puts His Holy Spirit in us. The indwelling Holy Spirit is the guarantee of our inheritance. The Word of God says,

> *"In him you also, who have heard the word of truth, the gospel of your salvation, and have believed in him, were sealed with the promised Holy Spirit, which is the guarantee of our inheritance until we acquire possession of it, to the praise of his glory"* (Ephesians 1:13-14).

> *"For all the promises of God find their Yes in him. That is why we utter the Amen through him, to the glory of God. But it is God*

who establishes us with you in Christ, and has commissioned us; he has put his seal upon us and given us his Spirit in our hearts as a guarantee" (II Corinthians 1:20-22).

"For while we are still in this tent, we sigh with anxiety; not that we would be unclothed, but that we would be further clothed, so that what is mortal may be swallowed up by life. He who has prepared us for this very thing is God, who has given us the Spirit as a guarantee" (II Corinthians 5:4-5).

You have the Holy Spirit in you. That is a guarantee that you will not perish. You have the life of God in you. You are eternal. God set out to prepare you for Himself that He might have you as a bride for His Son. Rejoice in this.

WHAT IF YOU FALL INTO SIN?

If you fall into sin, you should immediately confess the sin, forsake it, and keep going on with the Lord Jesus. The Bible says,

"If we say we have no sin, we deceive ourselves, and the truth is not in us. If we confess our sins, he is faithful and just, and will forgive our sins, and cleanse us from all unrighteousness. If we say we have not sinned, we make him a liar, and his word is not in us" (1 John 1:8-10).

If you enjoy sin and continue to practise it, you should rest assured that you are a child of the devil and will perish unless you repent.

SAVED. ETERNALLY SECURE IN CHRIST ANY RESPONSIBILITY?

To be eternally secure in Christ carries with it very serious conse-quences. The Bible says,

"He chose us in him before the foundation of the world, that we should be holy and blameless before him" (Ephesians 1:4).

Your election to salvation also includes an election to holiness and blamelessness. If you do not co-operate with the Holy Spirit of God so that He renders you holy and blameless in Christ, you will find out that your election to salvation is without meaning; for you are saved from sin. To continue to sin and proclaim your eternal security, is noise-making. You must be holy; for He who called you is holy.

You were ordained unto eternal life. You were also ordained unto good works. The Bible says,

> *"For we are his workmanship, created in Christ Jesus for good works,*
> *which God prepared beforehand, that we should walk in them"*
> (Ephesians 2:10).

You are saved for good works. You are predestined unto good works. You are destined to obey the Lord in all things. If the good works are not forthcoming, if your character is not increasingly resembling that of the Lord Jesus, and if there are no souls being brought into the Kingdom, nor an increasing prayer life, then you are most likely not a child of God, and this assurance does not apply to you.

God's grace to you must not be in vain. The apostle Paul said,

> *"For I am the least of the apostles, unfit to be called an apostle, because*
> *I persecuted the church of God. But by the grace of God I am what*
> *I am, and his grace toward me was not in vain. On the contrary, I*
> *worked harder than any of them, though it was not I, but the*
> *grace of God which is with me"* (I Corinthians 15:9-10).

To be eternally secure in Christ means that you determine to work harder for Christ than anyone else, yet you realise that it is not you working, but the grace of God in you. Praise the Lord!

WHAT IF YOU DOUBT YOUR SALVATION?

Doubts are from the devil. Resist them. Look unto the Lord Jesus. Look away from yourself. Trust the Lord Jesus. He has made definite promises concerning you. He will not change His mind. He will also help you not to change your mind. You have been born into His family. He will see you through. The devil will ask for you that he may sift you like wheat, but the Lord will pray for you, and the Father cannot say, "No," to any topic of His intercession. He loves you. He loved you while you were His enemy. He will not leave you now that you are His child. He has prepared a place for you. He will surely come and take you so that where He is, you may be also. Glory, glory, glory be to His name! He is wonderful. You, too, are wonderful in Him.

QUESTIONS

1. All true believers will enjoy eternal life in the end, does it matter now that they should have assurance of that fact?
2. Will someone who has assurance of full salvation not therefore become careless and not labour to please the Lord?
3. Can there be false conversions?
4. What are the characteristics of those whose conversion is false?
5. What are the marks of true conversion?
6. What was lacking in the rich young ruler?
7. How could he have made up for that deficiency?
8. Why was the Scribe not accepted by the Lord immediately he offered to follow Him?
9. Was the disciple (Matthew 8:21-22) totally committed to the Lord?
10. When is a person truly converted?
11. When did God first know you?
12. (a) When did He first ordain you unto salvation? (b) When did you personally receive your salvation from the Lord?
13. On what basis did He ordain you unto salvation?
14. What part have works to play in your salvation?
15. How far does God change the sinner at conversion?
16. Why can no one snatch you out of the hand of Christ?
17. The apostle Paul was confident about God's work in the lives of the Philippians and His capacity to bring it to an end. Are

you confident that the Lord will bring what He has started in you to a finish? Can He be depended upon to do this?

18. Write out the things that cannot separate you from the love of God in Christ Jesus.

19. Write out the things that are outside God's control and, therefore, will surely separate you from the love of God in Christ Jesus.

20. What is eternal life?

21. Do you have eternal life?

22. When did eternal life begin in you?

23. Is it possible that through some error on your part you lose your eternal life?

24. Does the Holy Spirit live in you?

25. What is He there for?

26. Can a believer sin?

27. Have you ever sinned since you believed?

28. What must you do if you fall into sin?

29. Do you cease to be saved if you fall into sin?

30. If you sin continually and enjoy it, does this confirm your salvation?

31. Outline three responsibilities of people whose salvation is secure in Christ.

32. What must you do if you doubt your salvation?

VERY IMPORTANT!!!

If you have not yet received Jesus as your Lord and Saviour, I encourage you to receive Him. Here are some steps to help you,

ADMIT that you are a sinner by nature and by practice and that on your own you are without hope. Tell God you have personally sinned against Him in your thoughts, words and deeds. Confess your sins to Him, one after another in a sincere prayer. Do not leave out any sins that you can remember. Truly turn from your sinful ways and abandon them. If you stole, steal no more. If you have been committing adultery or fornication, stop it. God will not forgive you if you have no desire to stop sinning in all areas of your life, but if you are sincere, He will give you the power to stop sinning.

BELIEVE that Jesus Christ, who is God's Son, is the only Way, the only Truth and the only Life. Jesus said,

> *"I am the way, the truth and the life; no one comes to the Father, but by me" (John 14:6).*

The Bible says,

> *"For there is one God, and there is one mediator between God and men, the man Christ Jesus, who gave himself as a ransom for all" (1 Timothy 2:5-6).*

"And there is salvation in no one else (apart from Jesus), for there is no other name under heaven given among men by which we must be saved" (Acts 4:12).

But to all who received him, who believed in his name, he gave power to become children of God..." (John 1:12).

BUT,

CONSIDER the cost of following Him. Jesus said that all who follow Him must deny themselves, and this includes selfish financial, social and other interests. He also wants His followers to take up their crosses and follow Him. Are you prepared to abandon your own interests daily for those of Christ? Are you prepared to be led in a new direction by Him? Are you prepared to suffer for Him and die for Him if need be? Jesus will have nothing to do with half-hearted people. His demands are total. He will only receive and forgive those who are prepared to follow Him AT ANY COST. Think about it and count the cost. If you are prepared to follow Him, come what may, then there is something to do.

INVITE Jesus to come into your heart and life. He says,

"Behold I stand at the door and knock. If anyone hears my voice and opens the door (to his heart and life), I will come in to him and eat with him, and he with me " (Revelation 3:20).

Why don't you pray a prayer like the following one or one of your own construction as the Holy Spirit leads?

"Lord Jesus, I am a wretched, lost sinner who has sinned in thought, word and deed. Forgive all my sins and cleanse me. Receive me, Saviour and transform me into a child of God. Come into my heart now and give me eternal life right now. I will follow you at all costs, trusting the Holy Spirit to give me all the power I need."

When you pray this prayer sincerely, Jesus answers at once and justifies you before God and makes you His child.

*Please write to us (**ztfbooks@cmfionline.org**) and I will pray for you and help you as you go on with Jesus Christ.*

THANK YOU

For Reading This Book

If you have any question and/or need help, do not hesitate to contact us through **ztfbooks@cmfionline.org**. If the book has blessed you, then we would also be grateful if you leave a positive review at your favorite retailer.

ZTF BOOKS, through the Christian Publishing House (CPH) offers a wide selection of best selling Christian books (in print, eBook & audiobook formats) on a broad spectrum of topics, including marriage & family, sexuality, practical spiritual warfare, Christian service, Christian leadership, and much more. Visit us at **ztfbooks.com** to learn more about our latest releases and special offers. **And thank you for being a ZTF BOOK reader**.

We would like to recommend to you the second book in **The Christian Way Series** - The Way of Obedience:

The truths in Book Two had very profound effect on my life. Since I received the Lord JESUS as my Saviour and Lord, I have felt in an increasing way that I was compelled to tell the whole world about His salvation.

When in 1970 the HOLY SPIRIT came upon me, ministry was given to me by the Lord for His Body. I would never have gone far without that indispensable anointing that took place in the

privacy of my room, on a Saturday afternoon, at 5 pm.

When in 1978, I bore testimony to my union with the Lord JESUS in water baptism, I got much of hell into violence, while heaven rejoiced.

In this book, by the grace of GOD, I present these three basic truths of baptism into water, baptism into the HOLY SPIRIT and witnessing as they are set forth in the Word of GOD.

This book goes out with prayer that it will bring all twice-born people into obedience on basic issues. May GOD the HOLY SPIRIT lead all its readers into immediate and continuous obedience.

Thank you and God bless you!

Zacharias Tanee Fomum

ABOUT THE AUTHOR

Professor Zacharias Tanee Fomum was born in the flesh on 20th June 1945 and became born again on 13th June 1956. On 1st October 1966, He consecrated his life to the Lord Jesus and to His service, and was filled with the Holy Spirit on 24th October 1970. He was taken to be with the Lord on 14th March, 2009.

Pr Fomum was admitted to a first class in the Bachelor of Science degree, graduating as a prize winning student from Fourah Bay College in the University of Sierra Leone in October 1969. At the age of 28, he was awarded a Ph.D. in Organic Chemistry by the University of Makerere, Kampala in Uganda. In October 2005, he was awarded a Doctor of Science (D.Sc) by the University of Durham, Great Britain. This higher doctorate was in recognition of his distinct contributions to scientific knowledge through research. As a Professor of Organic Chemistry in the University of Yaoundé 1, Cameroon, Professor Fomum supervised or co-supervised more than 100 Master's Degree and Doctoral Degree theses and co-authored over 160 scientific articles in leading international journals. He considered Jesus Christ the Lord of Science ("For by Him all things were created..." – Colossians 1:16), and scientific research an act of obedience to God's command to "subdue the earth" (Genesis 1:28). He therefore made the Lord Jesus the Director of his research laboratory while he took the place of deputy director, and attributed his outstanding success as a scientist to Jesus' revelational leadership.

In more than 40 years of Christian ministry, Pr Fomum travelled extensively, preaching the Gospel, planting churches and training spiritual leaders. He made more than:

- 700 missionary journeys within Cameroon, which ranged from one day to three weeks in duration.
- 500 missionary journeys to more than 70 different nations in all the six continents. These ranged from two days to six weeks in duration.

By the time of his going to be with the Lord in 2009, he had preached in over 1000 localities in Cameroon, sent over 200 national missionaries into many localities in Cameroon and planted over 1300 churches in the various administrative provinces of Cameroon. At his base in Yaoundé, he planted and built a mega-church with his co-workers which grew to a steady membership of about 12,000. Pr Fomum was the founding team-leader of Christian Missionary Fellowship International (CMFI); an evangelism, soul-winning, disciple making, Church-planting and missionary-sending movement with more than 200 international missionaries and thousands of churches in 65 nations spread across Africa, Europe, the Americas, Asia and Oceania. In the course of their ministry, Pr Fomum and his team witnessed more than 10,000 recorded healing miracles performed by God in answer to prayer in the name of Jesus Christ. These miracles include instant healings of headaches, cancers, HIV/AIDS, blindness, deafness, dumbness, paralysis, madness, and new teeth and organs received.

Pr Fomum read the entire Bible more than 60 times, read more than 1350 books on the Christian faith and authored over 150 books to advance the Gospel of Jesus Christ. 5 million copies of these books are in circulation in 12 languages as well as 16 million gospel tracts in 17 languages.

Pr Fomum was a man who sought God. He spent between 15 minutes and six hours daily alone with God in what he called Daily Dynamic Encounters with God (DDEWG). During these DDEWG he read God's Word, meditated on it, listened to God's voice, heard God speak to him, recorded what God was saying to him and prayed it through. He thus had over 18,000 DDEWG. He also had over 60 periods of withdrawing to seek God alone for periods that ranged from 3 to 21 days (which he termed Retreats for Spiritual Progress). The time he spent seeking God slowly transformed him into a man who hungered, thirsted and panted after God. His unceasing heart cry was: "Oh, that I would have more of God!"

Pr Fomum was a man of prayer and a leading teacher on prayer in many churches and conferences around the world. He considered prayer to be the most important work that can be done for God and for man. He was a man of faith who believed that God answers prayer. He kept a record of his prayer requests and had over 50, 000 recorded answers to prayer in his prayer books. He carried out over 100 Prayer Walks of between five and forty-seven kilometres in towns and cities around the world. He and his team carried out over 57 Prayer Crusades (periods of forty days and nights during which at least eight hours are invested into prayer each day). They also carried out over 80 Prayer Sieges (times of near non-stop praying that ranges from 24 hours to 120 hours). He authored the Prayer Power Series, a 13-volume set of books on various aspects of prayer; Supplication, Fasting, Intercession and Spiritual Warfare. He started prayer chains, prayer rooms, prayer houses, national and continental prayer movements in Cameroon and other nations. He worked with leaders of local churches in India to disciple and train more than 2 million believers.

Pr Fomum also considered fasting as one of the weapons of Christian Spiritual Warfare. He carried out over 250 fasts ranging from three days to forty days, drinking only water or water supplemented with soluble vitamins. Called by the Lord to a distinct ministry of intercession, he pioneered fasting and prayer movements and led in battles against principalities and powers obstructing the progress of the Gospel and God's global purposes. He was enabled to carry out 3 supra – long fasts of between 52 and 70 days in his final years.

Pr Fomum chose a lifestyle of simplicity and "self- imposed poverty" in order to invest more funds into the critical work of evangelism, soul winning, church-planting and the building up of believers. Knowing the importance of money and its role in the battle to reach those without Christ with the glorious Gospel, he and his wife grew to investing 92.5% of their earned income from all sources (salaries, allowances, royalties and cash gifts) into the Gospel. They invested with the hope that, as they grew in the knowledge and the love of the Lord, and the perishing souls of people, they would one day invest 99% of their income into the Gospel.

He was married to Prisca Zei Fomum and they had seven children who are all involved in the work of the Gospel, some serving as missionaries. Prisca is a national and international minister, specializing in the winning and discipling of children to Jesus Christ. She also communicates and imparts the vision of ministry to children with a view to raising and building up ministers to them.

The Professor owed all that he was and all that God had done through him, to the unmerited favour and blessing of God and to his worldwide army of friends and co-workers. He considered himself nothing without them and the blessing of God; and would have amounted to nothing but for them. All praise and glory to Jesus Christ!

facebook.com/cmfionline

twitter.com/cmfionline

instagram.com/cmfionline

pinterest.com/cmfionline

youtube.com/cmfionline

ALSO BY Z.T. FOMUM

Online Catalog: https://ztfbooks.com

THE CHRISTIAN WAY

1. The Way Of Life
2. The Way Of Obedience
3. The Way Of Discipleship
4. The Way Of Sanctification
5. The Way Of Christian Character
6. The Way Of Spiritual Power
7. The Way Of Christian Service
8. The Way Of Spiritual Warfare
9. The Way Of Suffering For Christ
10. The Way Of Victorious Praying
11. The Way Of Overcomers
12. The Way Of Spiritual Encouragement
13. The Way Of Loving The Lord

THE PRAYER POWER SERIES

1. The Way Of Victorious Praying
2. The Ministry Of Fasting
3. The Art Of Intercession
4. The Practice Of Intercession
5. Praying With Power
6. Practical Spiritual Warfare Through Prayer
7. Moving God Through Prayer
8. The Ministry Of Praise And Thanksgiving
9. Waiting On The Lord In Prayer
10. The Ministry Of Supplication
11. Life-Changing Thoughts On Prayer, Volume 1

PRACTICAL HELPS FOR OVERCOMERS

GOD, SEX AND YOU

RECENT TITLES BY THE ZTF EDITORIAL TEAM

PRACTICAL HELPS IN SANCTIFICATION

MAKING SPIRITUAL PROGRESS

1. Vision, Burden, Action
2. The Ministers And The Ministry of The New Covenant
3. The Cross In The Life And Ministry Of The Believer
4. Knowing The God Of Unparalleled Goodness
5. Brokenness: The Secret Of Spiritual Overflow
6. The Secret Of Spiritual Rest
7. Making Spiritual Progress, Volume 1
8. Making Spiritual Progress, Volume 2
9. Making Spiritual Progress, Volume 3
10. Making Spiritual Progress, Volume 4

EVANGELISM

1. God's Love And Forgiveness
2. The Way Of Life
3. Come Back Home My Son; I Still Love You
4. Jesus Loves You And Wants To Heal You
5. Come And See; Jesus Has Not Changed!
6. 36 Reasons For Winning The Lost To Christ
7. Soul Winning, Volume 1
8. Soul Winning, Volume 2
9. Celebrity A Mask

UNCATEGORISE

1. Laws Of Spiritual Success, Volume 1
2. The Shepherd And The Flock
3. Deliverance From Demons
4. Inner Healing
5. No Failure Needs To Be Final
6. Facing Life's Problems Victoriously
7. A Word To The Students

ZTF AUTO-BIOGRAPHIES

DISTRIBUTORS OF ZTF BOOKS

These books can be obtained in French and English Language from any of the following distribution outlets:

EDITIONS DU LIVRE CHRETIEN (ELC)

- **Location:** Paris, France
- **Email:** editionlivrechretien@gmail.com
- **Phone:** +33 6 98 00 90 47

INTERNET

- **Location:** on all major online **eBook, Audiobook** and **print-on-demand** (paperback) retailers (Amazon, Google, iBooks, B&N, Ingram, NotionPress, etc.).
- **Email**: ztfbooks@cmfionline.org
- **Phone**: +47 454 12 804
- **Website**: ztfbooks.com

CPH YAOUNDE

- **Location:** Yaounde, Cameroon
- **Email:** editionsztf@gmail.com
- **Phone:** +237 74756559

ZTF LITERATURE AND MEDIA HOUSE

- **Location:** Lagos, Nigeria
- **Email:** zlmh@ztfministry.org
- **Phone:** +2348152163063

CPH BURUNDI

- **Location:** Bujumbura, Burundi
- **Email:** cph-burundi@ztfministry.org
- **Phone:** +257 79 97 72 75

CPH UGANDA

- **Location:** Kampala, Uganda
- **Email:** cph-uganda@ztfministry.org
- **Phone:** +256 785 619613

CPH SOUTH AFRICA

- **Location:** Johannesburg, RSA
- **Email:** tantohtantoh@yahoo.com
- **Phone**: +27 83 744 5682

Made in the USA
Columbia, SC
15 April 2021